IN BAGGY BROWN BREECHES
and a cowboy hat

IN BAGGY BROWN BREECHES
and a cowboy hat

An Eastender's Wartime life as a Landgirl
in Kent

NORAH TURNER

Illustrated by David Moignard

MERESBOROUGH BOOKS
1992

Published by Meresborough Books, 17 Station Road, Rainham, Kent. ME8 7RS.

Meresborough Books is a specialist publisher of books on Kent. A list of books available at time of going to print can be found at the back of this book.

ISBN 0948193 654

Printed in Great Britain by Headley Brothers Ltd Ashford Kent and London

I dedicate this book with grateful thanks to
Pamela and John
without whose encouragement and support
it would never have got off the ground.

Chapter 1

My 'accidental' advent into the family was not greeted with over-whelming enthusiasm! I was not unloved, but I did make another body to fit into an already over-stretched household, and yet another mouth to be fed. Our house had seven small rooms, in which three families (twenty people) somehow existed, and this was about average for the slum area of Hackney in the East End of London in which it was situated.

Unemployment was rife, and even those who were fortunate enough to have regular jobs did not earn sufficient to make any sort of a splash. We had no point of comparison with the better-off and, had we ever thought about it (which of course we did not), we would have assumed that the whole universe lived in like manner. There was no television at that time, and we could not have afforded one of the 'new-fangled' crystal sets, even had they been readily available.

In the early years, my father had intermittent periods of being employed. He was a skilled glass-blower, and very clever with his trade. Some of the things he made were absolutely superb, but the primitive furnace needed to heat the glass for blowing only lasted a couple of months before the extreme temperatures caused its collapse, and it took a month of cooling down, re-building and bringing back to the correct heat again before it was put back into service. During these regular 'collapsed' periods my father was on the dole.

This was poverty enough, but when mechanisation reared its profitability head, the traditional methods went by the board, and all the old skilled workers went onto the ranks of the permanently unemployed.

Life was hard, to say the least, and, in spite of my mother's scrupulous fairness, and ingenuity, in making a little go a long way, we often left the table hungry.

Each time one of us children reached the age to leave school and begin to pay our way, the family's situation eased somewhat. It was

ironical that the young and unskilled had no difficulty finding work. Many employers, needing only unskilled labour, would opt for a factory full of school-leavers, they came so much cheaper!

When, at fourteen, I left school, I was able to start straight away in a factory making face-powder boxes. The work was not exactly mind stretching, I put lids on bases, by the thousands! It did, however, add a little more to the family budget, for my fifty-two hours a week produced the grand sum of ten shillings (50p today!).

My mother did as she had with all the others, taking eight of the precious shillings for my keep, putting one by to save for my clothes, and giving me back the grand sum of one shilling, all for myself!

Saturday night's visit to a local cinema, which cost ninepence, a twopenny piece of fish, and a pennyworth of chips, to eat on the walk home, saw off my entire pocket money for the week, but the cinema visits were a good investment, as those among the group I worked with, who had visited different venues, would recount every word of the dialogue, and describe every nuance of the action, in the particular programme they had seen, to keep the rest entertained while their hands performed their tedious tasks.

Our employers, the brothers Bright, exploited every means of squeezing out a little more profit, and the 'clocking-in system' was a prime example of their acumen. The clock, in a small shed, stood just inside the factory gate, and was overseen by a gate keeper to ensure no-one had the opportunity to clock in for another. With around 300 workers, queues were inevitable, and those towards the rear in these queues stood little chance of putting their card in the clocking device before the sounding of the factory hooter. For even a few seconds beyond that, the 'latecomer' would find her wages docked half-an-hour's pay, which, when we were all on such a tight budget, was quite devastating, but Catch 22 was in the ruling that everyone must be seen to be working once inside the gate, even the 'late' ones, who were not getting paid for the first half hour!

The Bright brothers were truly 'bright', and must have been having hysterics, all the way to the bank! There were no canteens in places of work in those days, and, in our factory, due to the strict rules of hygiene the buyers of our boxes insisted on, no food or drink was allowed to be consumed on the premises.

Most people could cope with going home for the half-hour break at mid-day, but those who had to bring packed lunches were not allowed to eat on factory soil, but had to stand, or sit, on the pavement outside its environs. Of course this mass exodus also involved the dreaded clocking out and in again, more queues, and more 'loverly' unpaid labour for the B.B.s!

This restricted life style was typical of the times for most young people. We were very unworldly, not even realising the extent to which we were exploited. We never had the opportunity to leave the slum areas, and had no idea that there WAS 'another half' living better than we did. In comparison with young people today, with their school trips all over and family holidays abroad, we were insular, inhibited and very ignorant.

The outbreak of the war, a source of foreboding to our elders (who remembered all too clearly the terrible times of the first one), just filled the youngsters' hearts with hope; this was surely the chance of adventure!

We soon found it sadly lacking, as young men and women that we knew were conscripted into the forces, and those too old for this were sent away to do munitions or other essential work. Our family, so recently appreciative of having enough food on the table, lost the experience again due to rationing.

But by far the most devastating of all was the Blitz! We found little 'adventure' in the nightly treks to the shelter in the back-yard. The only 'high' spots were our regular stints of street-corner fire fighting duty and, of course, the nightly toss-up to decide which one among us had the dubious pleasure of risking the bombs to go into the house for the sole purpose of making the last jug of cocoa, before the family settled down to another noisy night, stretched out on the mattresses.

Daytime air raids provided the workers at Bright's with much exercise and very little in the way of protection, especially those of us who worked nearest to the top. It would have been far too wasteful of working time for us to take shelter every time the sirens sounded, for the bombs might, after all, be dropped miles away! So a system of buzzers, connected to a switch on the roof, was installed all over the factory. A man who went onto the roof as soon as the siren went would press the buzzer, but not until enemy aircraft were actually in his sight, and then pressed again, for our own private little 'All Clear', as soon as the plane had passed over. Any number of times during the course of an alert, we would be marshalled into formation, and begin the descent of the eight flights of stone steps to ground level and the shelters, only to be halted part way, by the buzzer, and marched back up again. We could well have been the inspiration for 'The Grand Old Duke of York'! Luckily, a bomb never scored a direct hit on the factory; it would have been almost total carnage if one had.

Although I knew full well that putting lids on face powder boxes would not count as one of the 'reserved' occupations that excused some people from call-up, it still came as a bit of a shock when my age group was put on stand-by to register for service and, horror of horrors, the majority were destined for the W.A.A.C.s.

It would be almost impossible for the worldly-wise youngsters of today to imagine the innocence of their ilk in those pre-war days. There was no frankness (even between parents and children) on sexual matters, and the distorted versions of procreation, heard via the dirty joker or behind-the-hand sniggerer, had little accuracy!

It was through such unreliable channels that I learned 'The Truth' about the purpose of women being recruited into the forces — they were to be utilised as 'soldier's comforts'! I was not at all sure what this function would involve, but I was sure it could not be very nice, and I could not bear the thought of becoming one. It was during my frantic attempts to find a way out of it that I heard of the Women's Land Army.

Although I had never actually been in the countryside, I had vague recollections of it being quite pleasant, as we had passed through it in the charabanc on the Sunday School Treats when I was small.

Surely, I thought, it must be better to be out there than performing the unimaginable for the troops. When my instruction to register for service came through, I scuttled along to the nearest Land Army recruiting centre and volunteered.

The W.L.A. had no medical officers attached, so I had to obtain the certificate of fitness from my own doctor, and this was a drawback in my view. Those were the days when doctors remembered their patients without needing recourse to a secretarial note, and they knew families, and their circumstances (due, I suspect, to the need to know if they could afford to pay bills!).

My doctor had in mind what a seedy specimen I had been throughout my childhood, when he sat back in his chair and roared his derision at my request. "Work on the land!" he yelled, slapping his thigh, "It'll kill you!" But, as he nonetheless signed the precious certificate, "But, there again — it might eventually make a woman of you!"

The final interviewer at the centre was sceptical of my strength, even with the certification on the desk in front of her. She blathered on about the beef needed for hoisting potatoes onto lorries and skinning hefty great sheep until I felt sure she was going to turn me away. Eventually she did allow me to sign away my liberty, but, oddly enough, once I had set my name to it, the old gumph about the spuds on lorries and hefty sheep went right by the board!

I was to join an experimental gang, just four of us to begin with, to do a job that had never previously been tackled by women on a threshing machine. The good lady shook my hand vigorously and wished me luck with such fervour that a seed of doubt began to germinate in my mind, and I wondered, all the way home on the bus — What the heck WAS a threshing machine? and — Why had women never tackled it before? In just a couple of weeks I was to learn the answer to both these questions.

11

Moignard

Chapter 2

My mother was hoping that I would not be sent for too quickly, but in only a fortnight I received my orders. I was given a week's grace to give proper notice to Bright Bros., and get my affairs in order, before proceeding to Kent.

On the day my 'marching orders' came, my uniform was delivered, and what a puzzle that was at first! Mum helped me to unpack the brand new kit-bag, and the first items to come to light were a pair of real clod-hopping gum-boots (heavy wellies) and some giant-sized leather shoes. Mum muttered something about them supplying spare laces, but that did not register at the time, I was too busy rooting out more oddities. In all I had a heavy brown overcoat (three-quarter length), one fawn overall coat, and two pairs of dungarees, all in the same cotton drill material, three airtex short-sleeved shirts, green tie, three pairs of knee-length fawn socks, one bright green jumper, one pair of enormous baggy brown cord breeches, and one rather crumpled cowboy hat!

Giggling like a pair of school-girls, we set about putting it together in some sort of order for a dress rehearsal, and by the time I had actually got rigged out in it, we were quite helpless with laughter, I really did look a sight! Imagine if you can a skinny weed, with the normal London pallor and legs like match-sticks floating around inside those voluminous breeches, flaps dangling below the knees that we could not fathom out at all, the bulky jumper a good two sizes too big (all round) and that pantomime item, the cowboy hat!

Eventually we remembered the spare laces that Mum had been nattering on about and, with a fair bit of manoeuvering, we got the flapping legs of the breeches anchored in place under the socks. I could see, though, I was never going to qualify for any fashion show. Dressed in the full regalia, I felt like a clown, quite ridiculous, and I could not even think what it was going to be like to have other people seeing me in it. Mum shared my view, but my Dad, when he saw it, was thrilled to bits and so very proud of me.

At the outbreak of war, lots of parks and open spaces had been ploughed up to make allotments for people to grow their own vegetables and help out with the food shortages. A large area of marshland near us had been thus treated, and it had proved a real godsend to all the out-of-work men, in that they could feel they were doing something useful again. My Dad and his mates attacked their allotments with vigour and enthusiasm, but no proper tools, and very little know-how. Every house in our part of London had just a small square concrete yard at the back, and gardening experience was confined to the odd potted geranium on a window-sill. As soon as my Dad saw me in full sail he insisted on parading me before the whole allotment coterie, and he basked in the reflected glory of "My girl who's going away to work on the land."

The fateful day arrived all too soon, and it took every ounce of courage I had to step out along our familiar street, wave to Mum and Dad from the corner and begin the adventure of my life. I had never been away from home before and, quite frankly, I was terrified!

People turned to gape as I marched along in my resplendent colourfulness (the accent on the Fullness where my breeches were concerned). Those heavy shoes, so different from the cheap and flimsy high-heeled variety I usually favoured, were like ton weights to lift off the ground with each step, and sheer gravity forced them back to the pavement with a mighty crunch.

There were several hundred new recruits waiting on the platform at Waterloo station, all looking as awkward and bashful as I felt. We were checked off a list by a lady with a clipboard, and herded onto an already crowded train. There were always troops on the move, and civilians trying to carry on their normal business in spite of the abnormality of the war. We could not find seats on the train, and spent the entire journey perching awkwardly on our new kitbags in the corridor. W.V.S. ladies, at a stall outside the station at Tunbridge Wells, served us with weak tea and meagre sandwiches to fortify us after the wearisome train journey before we carried on. Then the lady with the clipboard hustled us onto coaches standing ready in the station approach, and we were away again. The coach windows had been blacked out and we could not see where we were being taken. The centre seating had been removed to make space for luggage, and we just sat, hour after hour, shy of starting conversations with complete strangers, acutely embarrassed if caught looking at someone across the heap of bags in the middle, and wishing like mad that we would soon arrive — somewhere!

Occasionally the convoy would grind to a halt and the clipboard lady, who led the coaches in a car, would do the rounds, calling names from her list. The ones called would sort their bags from the heap and disappear into the unknown, while the rest of us settled back, wondering how much further we had to go.

We had been in the coach for over three hours, and our numbers had dwindled to just four on the last coach, when we finally heard our names being called, all four of us. Cramped, hungry and very tired, we crawled out for our first glimpse of the rurals, and what a shock it was! We were in a long narrow lane that seemed to go on forever in either direction, enclosed by high untidy hedgerows. The only signs of humanity were a row of small dingy cottages that looked so uninviting that we could not believe we were going to live there.

Our billet was the one on the end, and our leader hustled us up the overgrown pathway. We had to go in via the back door as the front was almost obliterated by straggly rambler roses and tall weeds.

Our hosts had really put themselves out for the influx of four extra ration books (cynical as that may sound, we soon found it to be very close to the truth). Mr and Mrs Bundle had moved out of their bedroom to make room for as many beds as could possibly fit in. They had taken over the smaller, children's, room for themselves, and Mr Bundle had thrown together three very crude bunks in the tiny kitchen for their offspring. Our quarters were hardly in the laugh-a-minute category. We were furnished with a sagging double bed, two ancient iron camp-beds, a rickety washstand (basin on top, and tin bucket below), a cane chair minus its most vital element, the seat, and an upturned orange-box bearing one lonely candle in a saucer. Our 'wardrobe' was an ingenious arrangement of nails, hammered into every clear space on the walls and door. But the good lady told us our bedroom need only ever be for just sleeping in, as we would always be welcome to share the sitting room with the family in the evenings and at weekends.

After our leader (her name was Miss Howe) had left us, we unpacked our things, settling where we would sleep, as we got to know each other. The others all seemed to be nice, ordinary girls and, even at that early stage, it was obvious that we would be able to get on well together.

After all our journeying, and the stress of leaving home, we felt tired, disheartened and grubby. Perhaps things would appear in a more favourable light once we had cleaned up and got a decent meal inside us, we thought, optimistically. We now received our first real insight into the realities of the situation we were in. "You're not in London now, you know!" was the response of our hostess when we requested some hot water to freshen ourselves up. "We don't get all mod-cons in the country, I'm afraid you'll have to wait till I've cooked the dinner, and heated the kettle for the washing up, then there'll be room on the stove for a kettle for you, you will just have to get used to that, won't you?" And so it was, feeling tired, dirty, and dishevelled, we sat in our room until she called that the meal was ready.

When we had squeezed ourselves around the inadequate table in the tiny kitchen, along with Mr Bundle and the three children, Mrs Bundle served the food. Where oh where was that 'wholesome country cooking' we had heard so much about? We eyed our plates with dismay! two great wedges of suet pudding floundered beside some boiled potatoes and a small heap of yellowed cabbage, in a weak gravy that could well have been the water it had been cooked in! It looked quite revolting. We honestly tried to make some small inroad into this wet mass, but it really was too much, and we soon admitted defeat.

"I thought you'd be starving after the journey," our hostess fretted. "I suppose you don't want any afters, either?" When we saw what she was dishing up for Mr Bundle and the little ones, more of the beastly suet pudding, faintly disguised under a smear of jam, we hastily declined the offer, and when we had eventually been granted the coveted kettle of water, we were glad to retire to our room.

Over the ensuing weeks we were to discover that the dreadful pudding formed the basis of the Bundle diet, with slices fried for breakfast, and the invariable addition of wedges in the dinners and puddings. Mr Bundle, proudly extolling the virtues of his wife, explained that she made up one huge, salami shaped pudding wrapped in a cloth, and it was boiled in the wash boiler every Monday morning. As Mrs Bundle was a creature of habit who, regular as clock-work, did the whole family wash in one fell swoop on Mondays, it was a matter for much speculation among us girls as to whether the pudding went into the boiler before or after the dirty sheets. For the short time that we stayed there none of us ate a scrap of the monstrosity, so it was really immaterial how it was cooked.

The 'welcome' in the sitting room came a cropper from the first evening we sampled it. I think Mrs Bundle was afraid that having four 'attractive' girls in the place would bring a long-gone twinkle back into Mr Bundle's roving eye. She certainly took every opportunity to criticise his attempts at being civil to us, so, being quite convinced that our continuing presence in the sitting room would eventually bring about a major marital rift, we used our very genuine tiredness as an excuse to forego the 'pleasure' of their company, and retire to our cramped and far from cosy bedroom, to sit on our beds around the candle flickering in its saucer, and make brave attempts to write cheerful, reassuring letters home to our parents.

It was not that we expected too much. We had, after all, lived in cramped conditions at home, and food had always been a scarce commodity. But, in spite of the shortage of space in our home environment, things were geared as much as was possible to the comfort and happiness of all the occupants, and our mothers always went to great lengths to 'tart up' the sparsest of ingredients to make meals as appetising as was feasible.

At the Bundle house (now unanimously nick-named 'the Suets') very little effort was made on either count, and we realised quite early on that we were just four unwelcome necessities that had to be 'put up with' to achieve the extra money and rations.

Chapter 3

We found great difficulty sleeping that first night, for, adding to the discomfort of the beds and the hunger in our stomachs was an awful burning home-sickness that was quite devastating. Before we emerged from our room the next morning there was a general sur-reptitious dabbing at reddened eyes with cold water, that told its own story. Mr Suet was already munching into his breakfast when we entered the kitchen. The children were still asleep in their bunks, and there was a very strong (and pungent) indication of at least one wet bed. When we saw Mrs Suet, knife in hand, preparing to slice off more of the giant pudding to add to what was obviously her own allocation, already sizzling in the pan, we hastily eschewed any tendency to eat fried breakfast, and were, rather grudgingly, given a slice of bread and margarine apiece as a substitute.

On this, our first day, we were excused work as we had to go to 'The Yard' to introduce ourselves to the gaffer, and then pick up our bicycles from the station. It was a kind of 'lull before the storm' settling-in-day. The yard was just outside the village of Horsmonden, about two miles' walk from the Suet cottage, and the gaffer, a Mr Lamb, was a much bewhiskered old gent who, after looking us over thoroughly, grunted and then uttered in a dis-gruntled voice to no one in particular, "They promised me WOMEN! Just look what they've sent!" This, of course, did nothing at all for our egos, especially when his further instructions and injunctions meant so little to our unqualified ears.

We gazed in awe at the four huge steam engines, in various stages of refurbishment and raising steam. They were similar to ones we had seen steam rolling freshly tarred roads. We wondered if these could be what the country people called threshing machines, but Mr Lamb had already been so derogatory about our lack of stamina and experience that we dare not incur more of his scorn to enquire.

With a sense of foreboding we went on to our next call, the station. We were a mite apprehensive about the bicycles, as only

two of us had ever ridden before, the qualification not having been mentioned at our enrolment interviews. Amy had on occasion in her youth ridden her cousin's fairy cycle. I had, some time before, been given a derelict nurses' bike, much too big for me really, but, as it was confiscated almost straight away (I mentioned an ambition to ride to Southend on it!) this experience was not very comprehensive.

Dolly and Ellie had never even been on one and, when we spotted the four bikes leaning against the wall outside the station master's office an anguished groan rent the air, "Oh Please, let these NOT be ours!" I do not know what we had envisaged — something bright, newish looking, our size even! Our issue were huge, ex-post office bikes, red paint peeling and elements of rust showing beneath the chips. Oh! How we wished, at that moment, to be whisked back to the land of the good old bus stops!

For our first week, we had been told, we were to be fetched and brought home again by the 'farmer of the day'. This was to give us time to get used to the area, and learn some of the routes we would have to take to get to work. After this initiation we would be expected to ride everywhere under six miles from base. So, as well as all the other things we needed to acclimatise to, we had just one week of precious spare time, in the evenings and on the one weekend, to conquer these giant contraptions!

The area that we were in was very hilly, and, although a steep hill is somewhat of an aid to a beginner with regard to maintaining balance, it comes as a really bad shock when, unable to cope with the speed, the said learner comes a cropper at the bottom. I think every hill in the district around our village had a much-flattened clump of stinging nettles at its lowest point, a sort of 'Land Girls Were Here' graffito. We noted that nearly all hill bottoms were generously endowed with the beastly stingers, and often wondered if 'Someone up there' had a thing against learner cyclists!

We did manage to cope with the darned bikes by the end of our week's grace, and could sail along quite cockily on the flat bits. The hills were still a problem though, and we eventually came to a unanimous conclusion that somehow, and soon, we would have to find a way to slow down our unwieldy steeds before they reached the point of no return on these hills. We were to learn a quite ingenious way of doing this, but, for the moment, we just wished the dratted bikes had brakes!

Mrs Suet had provided each of us with a hunk of bread and cheese wrapped in newspaper, and a beer bottle full of cold tea between us for our midday break, and, clutching these, we sat in the back of the farm lorry that had been sent for us on the first morning. Shaking and swaying down endless miles of country lanes, it seemed we would never get anywhere, but eventually the lorry came to a halt beside a gate, and just inside it we got our first sight of a threshing machine. One of the big steam engines from the yard stood nearest to the gate into the field, puffing clouds of grey smoke and steam into the air like a great, black dragon. The machine itself stood beside a high corn stack, from which two men were removing thatch. The machine, several yards distant from the engine, but attached to it by a wide leather drive belt, was an awesome sight, all wheels, belts, and strange apertures, with chutes at the front end to which men were attaching sacks. At the rear end

was another strange machine that took up the entire width of the thresher and was positioned underneath a gaping hole in the back of it. This oddity was called a trusser.

Nowadays in the country you can watch a combine harvester trundling around a field as, in one single operation, it cuts the corn, threshes out the seed, spews the grain through a pipe into an accompanying container lorry, bales up the straw and leaves all the dust and broken straws on the ground in its wake. Before these marvellous machines were invented, however, harvesting was a very different kettle of fish. When the corn was ripe, the reaping machine went into the field, cut it, and bound it into heavy bundles, called sheaves. Farmhands followed the harvester, picking up the sheaves as they were dropped, and standing them in clumps of about eight, in a kind of pyramid arrangement, grain ears uppermost, to finish drying off. If it happened to rain on these 'stooks' everyone had to go back to the field to turn the sheaves about until it had all been well aired. It had to be thoroughly dry before it could be stacked, because damp straw, when compressed in the weight of a stack, quickly heats up, and either catches light or rots.

When all in the field was dried to the farmer's satisfaction, the horses and wagons were kept constantly on the go, dawn to dark, between the field and the site of the stacking, bringing in the sheaves in high loads to be built up into the stacks. This was a job to be got through as quickly as possible in case weather spoilt it before it was safety under cover. We had all sung the hymns about 'Bringing in the sheaves' in our Sunday School days, and now at last we had some idea of what it was all about. Once stacked and thatched against the weather, the corn was safe until the threshing contractor came on his rounds. On our first day on the farm we did not know any of this of course. We introduced ourselves to Bill, the steam engine operator, and Bert, the threshing machine expert, and, although you would never have guessed it from our cool reception, these two men were to become the best friends we would ever have.

Because of wartime food shortages, and restricted allocations of such labour as was available, the Ministry of Agriculture required farmers to do their utmost to preserve the corn in firm well-protected stacks, built like houses, and thatched against whatever weather came up, until it was their turn for some of it to be threshed. Each farm was allowed the services of the threshers for a short period only, we worked on a strict rota, and rarely spent more than three days on any one farm. With this rationing of our avail-ability, a farmer with several stacks of corn could cash in on one of them early in the season, but not see the final one going through the machine until March or April of the following spring.

Our parts in the operation were only occasionally varied, as we usually got the jobs the resident farm workers hated most, and that rarely varied from farm to farm. As a general rule, we would have the same four tasks. There would be one on top of the cornstack, pitching the sheaves down to the second girl, standing on the roof of the machine. This girl caught them (if the pitcher's aim was good) or picked them up from the deck and, with one hand grasp-ing the knot in the binding, she had to cut the string at a point just on the other side of the knot, retaining the string in her hand as she passed the now loose sheaf to Bert. Hanging onto the strings was an important part of the operation, as when we missed it the string could play havoc inside the whirling drum, and Bert would not have time to retrieve it as he skilfully fed the sheaf into the machine at a steady rate. It was quite a feat to do this job at the speed and rhythm required to keep the machine going to its full capacity. In the beginning we were terrified of the razor-sharp hooked blade that was secured, by a leather thong, round the bond cutter's wrist.

Bert stood in an oblong-shaped cut-out in the roof, which put him at just the right level to take the sheaf from the bond-cutter's hands and riffle it out into the thickness that the machine could best cope with. That was quite the most skilful, and the most dangerous, job of them all.

The third girl was positioned at the rear end, on the ground level, and her job was to take the bundles of straw as they rattled out of the trusser, and pitch them to one of the farmhands, who would be making them into another stack. Nothing went to waste in wartime, and this straw would probably be used for thatching, or for litter in the cow-barns, eventually converting into good manure.

The fourth task was by far the most unpopular with everyone, and we knew, wherever we went, that no farmhand was going to be daft enough to choose it. The corn husks, bits of broken straw, and accumulated dust so blithely left behind by the modern combine harvesters, piled up beneath the stationary thresher, as it poured out in a never-ending, choking cloud. One of us had to keep on raking it back out of the way or it would so easily clog up the works. But even with the long-handled rake provided, the cavel raker had to go right in close to the rocking, rattling machine, and was invariably smothered in the clouds of dust.

To make life easier, we agreed to share out the jobs and, at Bert's suggestion, changed over after every break so that we had roughly a quarter of each day on each job. This system helped us learn to be quite versatile in our ability to fill in on any job we might be required to do, but it did have one big disadvantage — we all finished work, at the end of every single day, looking exactly like chimney sweeps!

Chapter 4

We were all pure cockneys, with the kind of pre-war jobs that were no great strain on hands or muscles, coming from an area where there was bound to be a bus stop at the end of the road, and a cinema somewhere in the vicinity. Although we had no bathroom at home, there were always slipper baths attached to the swimming bath complex, where for a copper or two we could get a good hot bath on Friday nights, and between times hot water was not rationed in our homes. We could always wash ourselves, our hair, or our clothes, whenever we felt the need. We had taken these benefits so much for granted, we did not even realise they were there until we lost the lot in one fell swoop.

When we had finished an incredibly long hard day's work, and biked our weary way back to the house, our hands raw with broken blisters and every overstretched muscle screaming in protest at having been so abused, how we would have appreciated being able to pop into a soothing, warm bath, or even have a wash, to rid our clogged pores of all the accumulated dirt of the day, before we sat down to an appetising, nourishing meal. That, however, was a pipe dream! The reality was a cramped room with a solitary candle, a shared kettle of water at Mrs Suet's convenience, and another meal of ghastly stodgy pudding.

Our two workmates, who watched our early struggle to come to terms with the work with some scepticism, began to show signs of respect when they realised that we were sticking at it and, very slowly, getting it right. We were still somewhat of an unknown quantity to them, and, wary of seeming too eager to accept us, they dropped helpful hints in a very oblique way, so that we could not thank them.

One day, when Bill had noticed Dolly mopping blood from her raw hands in her lunch break, he gazed intently at some cows in the next field as he said "'Tis really odd the way some people hang on to pitchfork handles, you'd think them pitchforks was alive and trying to gallop off." When we went back to the machine to start work, we caught Bert rubbing engine grease on the handles, muttering under his breath that it would do a power of good to anyone likely to have sore hands.

In this off-handed fashion they taught us the best way to climb the roof of a cornstack to remove the thatch, the most effective way to catch a sheaf, and how to use the knife safely. There were so many ways to make our jobs easier to cope with, and improve our efficiency at the same time, and all were passed on under the heading 'to save Bill and Bert having to pick up the pieces'. We were very grateful for their help, however they chose to give it, and took no offence at the references, frequently made, to our lack of know-how — it was kindly meant, and true.

The best of all the lessons, however, was teaching us how to laugh at ourselves, and find some grain of humour in even the most humiliating of our mistakes.

By the end of the first month we were beginning to work together as a team, our blisters were hardening off and turning into much less painful calluses. Our muscles were beginning to accept the constant abuse with more tolerances. It did not all come right at once, of course, but on the work front as a whole, things were looking brighter for us.

We were even getting better at riding our bikes, and only once in a while having a spill. The only fly in the ointment ws Mrs Suet's establishment, and we were really cheesed off with that.

Our only local contact with the Land Army was Miss Howe, who had escorted the coaches on that day we arrived in Kent. She had given us her phone number on that day with firm instructions to "Get in touch immediately if you have any queries — yes indeed! Any query or problem at all, after all, that is what I'm here for." Except that she was not. When we needed her advice so badly, our two and a half mile rides to the phone box were unfruitful, she was never there.

The final straw for us came one day when we finished early at one farm, but Bill calculated that by the time we had dismantled, and hitched everything up, got the show on the road to the next location, and got it all ready to function again, it would be too late to make a start that day. So, after we had helped with the packing up he let us go off early. That was how we came to arrive an hour before we were expected, and walked in on a truly sickening sight. The kitchen table had been laid for our evening meal, but obviously seeing she had time in hand, the good lady had pushed the cutlery to one side, and all three of the children sat in a row on the table as she raked through their hair, in turn, with a fine tooth comb. The local school was currently having a problem with infestation ("It's all those dirty little evacuees of course") and the family 'Suet' were thoroughly engrossed in the flea safari, right there on our dining table.

Needless to say, we did not even pretend to eat anything that evening, and frantically tried to contact Miss Howe again. Once again the long bike ride was to no avail, Miss Howe was still among the missing. I think we all reached the uttermost depths that night.

Bill and Bert had both been enquiring around their respective villages to see if someone would take us on. They knew we weren't happy at the Suets and guessed, by the way we were always scrounging any fruit or spare food on the farms, that we were not being fed too well either. The morning after the delousing spectacular, we turned up for work in deepest gloom. "Hey, come on now," Bill chided, "Let's see some smiles for a very good mate who's found a nice new billet for you!" We felt like hugging the dear man, even though it would have embarrassed him to death if we had. For the rest of the day we were on cloud nine and much too impatient to waste time going back to Suetville to clean up before going to see the lady. We went straight from work, in our dirty and dishevelled state.

She was a cuddly lady, plump to the point of fatness, and with a cheerful smile. Her name was Mrs Bird, and she welcomed us into her home with a mug of steaming tea and a hearty wedge of home made bread and butter each. It was enough to make us wonder if we had died and gone to Heaven!

The good lady seemed worried that we would be put off by the rules and regulations she had to lay out for us, if we agreed to go and live there. She was not very nimble on stairs and we would be expected to keep our rooms tidy (plural rooms!), to carry our water upstairs ourselves, and do other things like washing up, fetching water from the pump in the yard and so on. She insisted that we went up to look over the bedrooms in spite of our fears of spreading our dust around. She was quite undaunted by our messy appearance, "I've brought up a family of hulking great sons and am quite used to mucky farmers," she said.

The weekend saw us loading all our gear onto our bikes, as we said our heartfelt goodbyes to Suetville, with all its discomforts, and moved into our own lovely conception of sheer bliss on the outskirts of Lamberhurst. There were just two of us to each of the large bedrooms, with proper comfortable beds, an oil lamp apiece and downstairs a cosy sitting room, with a big Aladdin lamp to read by and a roaring log fire if we needed it. With whatever hot water we could lug up the stairs, and good wholesome food cooked by a born carer who had missed having someone to enjoy it, we knew we had landed on our feet.

Miss Howe came roaring in like the original white tornado when the news of our move filtered through to her. I think she felt guilty about not being available when we really needed her and, when she realised how much more central to our round of farms we were, she calmed down somewhat.

It was obvious that wild horses would be needed to drag us back, so, although still cross at us for "Letting a good lady down!" (meaning Mrs Suet we presumed), she let the new arrangement stand and left in a positive dither over "Having to apologise for people's bad manners!" We heard, much later, that the Suet's home had become very much akin to a transit camp, as, like us, new recruits were sent there and stayed only as long as it took them to find somewhere else. Poor Miss Howe must have spent a fair proportion of the war apologising to the pudding pushers.

Meanwhile, happy, and well looked after by Mrs Bird, we could really settle down and turn our energies to making a go of it at work.

Chapter 5

It was early in September that we first noticed the line of adjoining sheds, in a field next to the one we were threshing in. The farm men taking a wagon load of the newly threshed straw over to them roused our curiosity. The sheds were quite ugly, just a door (no windows), to each, with a corrugated iron roof and all were painted, or creosoted, a drab matt black. The farm men went along the row with their wagon full of trusses and, opening each door as they came to it, they tossed in a few trusses, then closed the door, and went on to the next shed.

We were removing the thatching on the last stack while they were doing this, and we asked the thatcher, who was helping us, what the sheds were for. He looked at us pityingly, as he explained, in a terse, country economy of speech, "Them piggerzootz o' course!" This was just about as informative to us as a description of hot weather to an Eskimo, but by this time, beginning to realise how much of our ignorance was already on display, we just nodded, agreeing knowledgeably, "O' course."

We speculated among ourselves on what exactly a piggerzootz was. It must obviously be the particular breed name of an animal we already knew, like the Longhorn in cattle, but what animal? We looked at the huts again and decided a horse was too tall for those doors, while only a very skinny cow would be able to squeeze through. The first part of the name made it almost a certainty that we were talking about some kind of pig. Having settled this in our minds, we concentrated on the work in hand, and forgot about the sheds, only occasionally thinking to glance across, for some sign that the animals had been installed. The sheds and the field were still unoccupied when we finished off the stack, packed up the machinery, and moved on.

It was nearly a week later when, upon arriving at a new farm in the dim light of a misty morning, we heard a truly nostalgic sound, or rather, a cacophony of sounds. There was the shrill chatter of excited children at play, coming from the far side of a small copse

28

of trees, and these were interspersed with loud harangues from adults: "Give yer sister back er welly, you little devil Erbert!" and "Shut up Ginny, sno good cryin ter me cos e's bit yer — bite im back!" These were sounds we'd grown up with, and could never have expected to hear in this rural wilderness.

As was usual, we had to get stuck in straight away on our preparations, the unpacking, the thatch removal and the eventual involvement in the threshing operation, so it was not until the dinner break that we had the opportunity to investigate the phenomenon of the cockney voices. The copse was the obvious venue for our mid-day penny spend, and it was just a few steps through to the other side of it.

The row of black sheds was almost identical to the one we had seen on the other farm. The doors were all closed and padlocked, and it was as quiet as a ghost town in a Western movie! But, people had been here — the ashes of a huge fire still lazily wafted blue smoke into the air. The grass was well-littered with sweet wrappers, crusts of bread and bits of broken toys. But it seemed the inhabitants of the little colony had moved on and we felt quite sad. This regret proved unnecessary as we could hear them long before we reached the scene of our operations the next morning, but when we went to look for them at mid-day, once again we found the encampment desolate in its emptiness.

It had been a fine, clear day and when at 5.30 there was only about half an hour's work left in the cornstack, it was still light enough for Bill to decide that we might as well work on and get it finished. Bill reckoned that, by getting it done, and the machine etc. packed up ready to move that day, he and Bert could come out and trundle on their way to the next farm first thing in the morning. It would take them some considerable time to transfer as our next call was right on the perimeter of our round, and although that meant we would have longer bike rides to work while we were there, it also gave us a bit of a lie-in on the first morning, while Bill and Bert were on the road.

It was entirely due to our working later that day that we finally got to see the owners of the mystery morning voices. The noise of the threshing machine, and the puffing and rattle of the engine, acted like a magnet to those noisy cockney kids. Wide-eyed they peered at us through the poles in the fence of their field. Dirty little urchins, in tatty clothes, well bespattered with mud: there must have been at least twenty of them, all sorts and sizes.

It was my turn at raking out the cavel and I could hear their speculations — "Whats she doin dyer reckon?" one tiny tot asked. "Playin sand castles, thats wot," answered the bigger boy standing next to her, while a girl, further up the fence, chimed in, "Dont be dafter an yer can elp, Arry, she's looking fer somefink she lost!" and, calling across to me, "Vats right innit missus?"

I asked them, between rakeouts, what they were doing on a farm out in wild and woolly West Kent. One of the women arrived at that moment, to sort out 'Arry and 'Erbert. She told me they were there for a month, "For the oppin." They came every year, as had their mothers before them, "To give the kids a bit of fresh air, an a bit of an oliday," which they could not otherwise afford. By coming for the hop picking they earned enough for their keep, so, in effect, their 'oliday' was free.

We found ourselves invited for a cup of tea with them when we had finished. As we were already so late we felt a few minutes more would make little difference to our dinners. The camp fire blazed in the evening dimness, giving a healthy glow to the faces of the people sitting in a circle around it.

All the farms seemed to have an orchard, and there was usually at least one tree that was diseased, or unfruitful, to be cut down and replaced. When the farmer also grew hops, he would make use of these trees by having them sawn into logs, and the logs stacked or heaped somewhere handy to the huts for the pickers' fires. An iron bar, suspended across the fire by a triangular support on either side of it, was equipped with hooks for the pickers' billy cans, and a long metal fork-like gadget could reach across the flames and remove a can without disturbing the rest. It was a primitive and very restrictive means of providing sustenance and, by the smells coming from the cans, they were all having stews of one sort or another for the evening meal.

Maggie, the one who had invited us, introduced us to the other women, who were all old friends from the same district in London, who travelled down together in the same lorry, and picked hops on the same farm, year after year. Each took the same hut every time and, after our cuppas, we were taken on a tour of them. We were amazed at the effort that had gone towards making the maximum comfort in such mediocre accommodation. Over half the width of the hut was taken up by a wall to wall platform, about two feet off the floor. The straw from the trusses, spread all over this, was the 'bedding' provision. But over the years extra comforts had been brought down from London; mattresses lay side by side on top of the straw layer, there were pictures on the drab walls, ornaments on every ledge, mats on the floor and bright curtains at the doorways. As each family retained the same hut they left their touches of comfort packed up at the end of each picking season, and the farmer would keep it locked up safely until the next season.

Many of the husbands, managing alone at home during their working days, came down for the weekends, and village shops, and the local pubs, had a heyday providing for these hungry families and ever-thirsty adults.

Hop pickers still go to the farms, but it is not the same these days. Then, each family was allocated a 'bin' which was constructed of strong sacking supported by a wooden frame, with handles at each end for easy moving from hill to hill as the bines were picked. Each bin was started off at one end of a row of hops, and the pickers worked their way up it, pulling down the bines and picking off the hops as they progressed, leaving behind them a devastated waste of stripped bines on the ground. The farm manager, or the boss himself, came round at intervals with a bushel basket, to measure out what each bin contained. He would scoop out the bushels and tip them into a container to be transported to

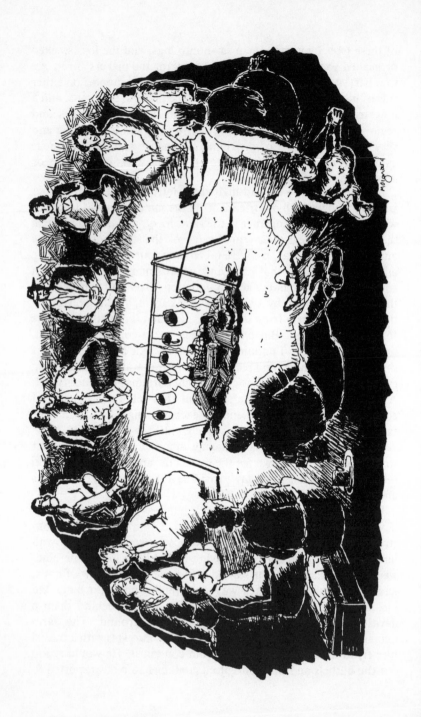

the oast houses, and would note down how many basketfuls he had taken from each bin, as payment was on the piece-work basis, an agreed amount for each bushel picked.

On present day farms tractors work through the hop gardens pulling specially equipped trailers and men cut off the hop-bearing part of the bines and hang them on the racks on the trailers. When fully loaded these are transported to a barn-like shed, where a machine carries the bines up and through a mechanical picker. Today's 'pickers' are more akin to production line workers as they stand beside a floor length belt carrying the picked hops along towards the waiting oasthouse attendants. All the pickers do is pick out leaves and bits of bine which have broken off with the hops. Even the drying off in the oasts has progressed beyond recognition. The coke or anthracite fuelled fires needed constant attention, and being an 'Oastie' meant having a bed in the oast, and sleeping in 'watches' between stoking the fires and turning the hops in the kilns. Oil, gas, electricity and computerisation have transformed the process into a precision operation undreamed of in the past.

Before we left the camp, we asked the Londoners how they got on with the countryfolk, and were dismayed to hear that on this farm at least semi-segregation was the norm. The Londoners were all set to work at one end of a hop garden, while the home workers (labourers' wives and other locals) would be started at the other end, which meant that the twain did eventually meet but only as they finished in the middle.

These hospitable, friendly Londoners took a dim view of 'stuck up yokels' and, I fear, the 'yokels' had the same attitude to them. As one old boy (of the same era as our old thatcher had been) told us, "Theys dirty, theys noisy, and ee caint unnerstand theys queer lingo!" We looked at each other and giggled as we thought of the 'piggerzootz', which we only now recognised as meaning 'pickers' huts'.

It was amazing that tribes living within fifty miles of each other should have so little in common, and barely speak the same language.

Chapter 6

Finding our way about to the different farms was a problem of nightmare proportions at first. Used as we were to clearly signed streets and districts, these twisting and turning narrow lanes, with side lanes running off in every and any direction, were a veritable maze. The area was to the east of Tunbridge Wells and included the villages of Pembury, Matfield, Brenchley, Horsmonden, Goudhurst, Lamberhurst, Frant and Wadhurst.

All signposts had been removed, or painted over, at the onset of war, to make progress more difficult for any invading force, we were told. It might or might not have confused the enemy, but it certainly left us right up the creek most of the time during our early months.

Bill and Bert were not too much help either, when we needed to report to a totally unknown farm the next day, for they would give us the location in what seemed to us a foreign language. Among their strange expressions, the most puzzling then were 'the four wents', the 'three wents' and the 'overwents'. Bill would tell us, "You take the short sharp shoot at the three wents, and then the overwent at the four wents," and Bert would add, "You'll see the farm out afore you when you're at the next wents."

It took us ages to pin them down to a proper explanation of these quaint terms, but we did eventually learn that a three wents was a T-junction, a four wents was a crossroads, and going overwents was to cross straight over at a crossroads; simple, according to their reckoning. We discovered that the 'went' had been in constant use when ploughmen had to walk behind a horse up and down a field. Up one row and back to where they had started from was a went. Please do not ask what possible connection this had with crossroads and T-junctions — we could not fathom it out ourselves. But to Bill and Bert's country minds it was totally logical.

We often met army personnel faced with the problem of trying to locate themselves and, on one occasion, directed a red-faced officer in a large armoured vehicle which was miles off course. We had lost our way several times on the morning of our first visit to a farm near the outskirts of Tunbridge Wells, and were very relieved to see the farm name at last on a gate. We turned into the farm approach, which was a twist and turn affair, heavily wooded on either side, so that we had to rely on our ears to register if other traffic was approaching each blind corner.

What we had not expected to come upon was about a dozen young children, spread right across the road, as we swept round one of the sharp bends. With no verges to turn off to, we had no choice, it had to be them or us, and how could we possibly have eliminated the entire infant population of the farm? Not one of us escaped damage either to herself or her bike, but thanks be, the children went unscathed.

It was as well that we were not expecting any comment on our self-sacrificial feat, for no tiny "Thank you" or "Are you O.K.?" was to be heard. They solemnly, and carefully, walked around the untidy heap of alien bodies and machines that was littering their path, without uttering a word, and carried on up the lane, presumably to catch the school bus. We arrived at the farm dishevelled and late, but the farmer forgave us when we had explained the circumstances. He told us that the various parents were always trying to impress on their broods the need to walk on one side of the lane in case they met anything going the other way, but, he said, they so rarely met any traffic, that they soon forgot to be careful. We were pleased to have the gratitude of these parents, who came back early from their dinner especially to fix up our bent bikes, so we could ride them home that night. We had still found no really reliable means of slowing down our brakeless broncos, but it was as we were leaving this very farm that we finally cracked it.

In those early days of not knowing our way about the area, it was a relief when we happened to finish at a farm in time to move on and start at another on the same day, because then we did not have to worry about finding the new farm, we just followed the procession.

It was quite a sight to behold when we packed up the whole kit and caboodle to travel. There would be Bill driving the steam engine at the head, with, hitched on behind, the threshing machine, the box caravan, and, at the rear, the old trusser, trailing wisps of straw along the road.

Bert on his bike, acted as chief marshal (following close behind to make sure that nothing vital fell off), and we would be the 'tailend Charlies', like the proverbial dustcarts that follow the Lord Mayor's Show, and it was while we were progressing slowly out of the farm gate, that Ellen noticed Bert's ancient old bike.

The men were always on site by the time we arrived for work and, as we were always first to leave at the day's end, we rarely saw him actually on it. It was quite out of the blue, then, when Ellen suddenly pointed at him, riding ahead of us and shouted, "Hey look, Bert's got no flipping brakes either." At first we felt she had to be joking, since Bert had superb control, even slow-riding as now, and on steep hills he had no problems at all.

As soon as we were on a straight bit of road, we caught up with him and asked how it was done. "That's something I larned when I was a little sprout," he chuckled. "When I wants to slow 'er down, I just brings 'er to 'eel." We watched as he brought the pedals into a horizontal line, which brought the heel of one of his boots level with the tyre of the rear wheel, and, as he gently put pressure on the side wall of the tyre, it had the same effect as a proper brake pad.

It was hardly the sort of manoeuvre that could be perfected straight off, and we had several near calamities before we learned to get the pressure just right for each different set of circumstances, but it gave us something to work at, and it was extremely gratifying when, over the following few months, we got the 'Heel-on-wheel' technique down to a fine art.

38

Chapter 7

Up until now I have not mentioned going home, and this is because we did not go very often. At first, when we were raw, sore and homesick, we could not trust ourselves, realising all too well what a shock it would give our parents to see us in such a state, and we knew they would try to persuade us to give up. We were more afraid of ourselves though. It would not, at that stage, have taken much persuasion to make us leave, which would have brought us right back to square one, with no other option but the army. Our other reasons for not going were the obvious ones of finance and opportunity. We were far from highly paid, and a sizable chunk of what we did earn had to be the statutory payment to our landlady for our keep, so each trip home was the result of very careful management of our money.

We worked until four o'clock on Saturdays, and the last bus, our only means of getting out of the village, left at a quarter to seven. After finishing work, helping to pack up the gear, biking back to the billet, and having the very necessary wash and change of clothing, there was so little time that we usually had to start out without a bite to eat. If we were lucky and caught the bus, we would arrive in Tunbridge Wells with barely time to spare to get another 'last', the Greenline to Lewisham. The Greenlines were ordinary double decker buses that did the long runs, like the inter-city coaches of today.

From Lewisham our ways diverged and I went on alone, a single decker through Blackwall Tunnel and then a double decker from Bow to Hackney. It was quite a trek, and always the possibility loomed of missing one of the connections and getting stranded at any stage. After so much chopping and changing I was always filled with relief finally to arrive, around ten o'clock, tired and hungry.

On Sunday morning the talking never stopped, with so much news to catch up on and so little time to do it in. 'Last' buses left so early that it would be time to start the long haul back soon after we had had our lunch. On my very first visit home, my Dad just could not wait to get me round to the allotments. All his mates had turned out specially to hear how I was getting on and, funnily enough, to ask my advice on their many and varied gardening problems!

They were of course as totally ignorant of threshing operations as I had been, and I had not the heart to throw cold water on their firm belief that my three months' 'experience' on the land had given me a complete education on the raising of crops, the treatment for blight and so on. I felt much too flattered at this attention — in those days it was not at all the done thing for menfolk to ask advice of women, especially when the said women were little more than teenagers. I advised, freely and with as much authenticity as I could muster, while keeping my fingers firmly crossed behind my back, hoping that this would not be the beginning of a blight on their efforts.

This incident brought home to me how very insecure these men felt, and how completely out of their depth they were in this gardening effort. From then on I started to listen in to the conversations of the men on the farms, who often discussed the progress of their own gardens. Most country people seem to be born with a very ample complement of green digits, they all have enormous gardens and keep their families in fresh vegetables and fruit. So with a fair amount of listening in, and the judicious asking of key questions, I was soon in a position to pass on useful tips to our gallant band of allotmenteers.

One of the treats from my childhood days was to visit Petticoat Lane with my father on Sunday morning, so when on my second trip home he suggested a quick dash up to 'the Lane' I jumped at the chance. Mum, Dad and I got up early and went off in fine fettle.

In those days it was quite a famous market, and usually crowded with cockneys after a bargain, but the war had brought many foreigners to our shores and a fair proportion of them were in the Lane on that Sunday. It was fascinating to see so many different uniforms and listen to the gabble of languages, the nasal twang of the Yanks and Canucks, the Aussie and New Zealand versions of English, and all the 'Free fighters', French, Dutch, Polish and many others, mixing incongruously with the cockney jargon of the stallholders.

Everyone tried to be helpful to these soldiers, sailors and airmen, although, in those days, before working people were paid for holidays, and only the very rich could afford to go abroad, they were more like creatures from outer space to most of us.

Mum and Dad had something specific that they wanted to buy, and as it was not exactly a riveting purchase, I wandered on to another stall, where a large, very voluble man was selling 'give-away' watches. The dust of the threshing had played havoc with mine and I hoped the 'give away' price would be low enough for me to buy a new one. It was while I was sorting through the money in my hand to see if I could run to it, that an enormous fist came from behind, and a gruff cockney voice, speaking slowly, and exceptionally clearly (as if talking to a child) separated the coins on my palm with the injunction, "This big 'un's alf a crown, the littler 'un's two bob, and you want one a them smallest ones as well." It dawned on me then, he thought I was one of the foreigners! The Land Army uniform was not an everyday sight in London, and it was quite obvious he had never seen one.

I had not the heart to disillusion him after his kind attempts to help, and anyway, it was fun to play along. So I thanked him for his advice, in what I fondly hoped was 'broken English' as I bought the watch with the coins he had pointed out. As he stepped jauntily away he had the manner of one who has done his good turn for the day. I had this vision of him arriving home, and telling the missus, "You won't berlieve it! them foreigners are sendin' girls over 'ere now, I jest 'elped one of 'em buy a ticker darn the Lane."

One of my weekends home was in the middle of winter, and the snow began to fall during the Saturday night. It carried on through into Sunday, and was quite heavy when it was time for me to start back. The London buses were running more or less normally, snow tends to get to the slushy stage fairly quickly in towns, but, once the Greenline got onto country roads, it became very tricky indeed. The verges at the roadside were invisble under deep drifts, and it must have been extremely difficult for the driver to see where the road actually was. There were about a dozen passengers left when, on the last lap, the bus skidded round a sharp bend, and careering off the road altogether, finished its journey half buried in a deep snowdrift!

All of us got off and tried to dig it out with whatever came to hand, but it took so long (over an hour) before, at last, the driver was able to back out onto the road and get us moving again, that we knew we had missed the last buses from Tunbridge Wells to whatever villages each of us wanted to go on to.

41

Most of the other passengers were local people, used to this situation with the wartime bus and train deficiencies, and had alternative arrangements already to hand, relatives or friends living in or close enough to the town to offer shelter overnight, and one by one, they went their separate ways, until all that were left were myself and a gawky young soldier.

He told me his tale of woe as we stood indecisively at the now deserted bus stop. His unit had moved on while he had been away on leave and, although he knew it by name, he had no inkling of the location of the new camp. All would have been O.K. of course, if the snow had not stopped the trains running, he had the usual rail-pass and could have gone almost to the gate of the barracks. When someone at the station had told him of the bus-link alternatives, he had jumped on it, but of course, with the link broken, he was completely lost. When I elicited exactly where the camp was, and realised it was situated in the village beyond mine, I suggested that we start to walk, and hope to get a lift at least part of the way.

The few people who were allocated petrol rations to keep their cars on the roads were usually fairly generous about sharing this blessing, especially with service personnel, and it was not risky giving or accepting lifts, as it is today. We only saw one car, but although its driver, a doctor, did stop and offer us a ride, he was due to turn off at the next crossroads, just a few hundred yards on, and it was no help to us at all.

I think that thirteen miles was quite the longest that I have ever been called upon to slog. It was pitch dark, and there were no lights showing from the houses of farms we passed along the way, for the blackout would have effectively quelled them even had there been anyone still up at this late hour, but, of course, the further we progressed along the way the less likely that became. It was bitterly cold and, with no light, virtually impossible to distinguish between the road and the verge (or ditch) beside it. Our feet were soaked as we stumbled in and out of drifts along the wayside, and we talked, to try to pass the time, and help us on the way. The lad was getting more and more worried, as the time drew on. He should have reported back by midnight, and he feared that excuses about non-running trains and stranded buses would not carry much weight with his commanding officer.

It was twelve-thirty when I finally got back to Mrs Bird's, very, very tired and footsore. Although I knew I had a hard day ahead with only a few hours to sleep before the call at five-thirty, I felt really sorry for that young soldier. He still had four weary miles to walk after I had set him on the right road from our village, and goodness knows what penalties to pay for being so late.

Chapter 8

Autumn 'happened' to us soon after we made our debut into the country life style, and we were totally enraptured by the beauty of it.

The seasons, as such, had not meant all that much to us, apart from knowing that the winter was usually colder than summer. In London the year was divided by the four Bank Holidays, Easter, Whitsun, August and Christmas. We were about to learn how seasons were experienced by country folk.

We felt that Autumn must be the most beautiful time of all that first year. The colours in the woods were gorgeous, like a thousand different versions of the same flame. We picked a selection of the leaves to send home, longing to share the wonder of them with our parents, but they lost their glow before we could even think of getting them into the post.

We 'discovered' blackberries in the woods, and braved the discomforts of picking them. They were new to us, we had never seen them being sold in our street markets. Finding nuts that grew on trees and not market barrows was something to enthuse about, and we sated ourselves on this wonderful free of all! The locals irritated us with their amused tolerance of our enthusiasm, they thought we were soft in the head to get so 'het up' about something that they had seen every year of their lives, and just could not seem to take it in that we had not.

When Winter set in, although it had its own kind of beauty, especially when the frost and snow gave everything a shiny, crackly, look, it did tend to go over our heads that first year, for we had other things on our minds, and keeping ourselves warm was by far the most urgent.

It was not the fault of the Land Army that our uniform was so inappropriate for our particular requirements. I imagine for most ordinary farm work it must have been adequate, but with all the clambering about on cornstacks, in barns and on ladders, and the twisting and bending, the heavy greatcoat would have been much too restricting for us. The breeches, although baggy of seat, were tight round the legs and, being corduroy cloth, would have picked up every strand of loose straw, and clung to it. So we were left with our short-sleeved aertex shirts, woollen jumpers that also collected straw unless worn under our coats and the cotton drill dungarees and over-all coat. Consequently we found weathering our way through that first winter a battle for survival. I had never in all my life felt so perished with cold as I did then, especially in the January and February when there were heavy falls of snow.

As well as the thresher and trusser, part of our entourage was an old wooden box-caravan, of the type sometimes used by roadmen. This one's presence with our gear had originated in the days when the round was much more widespread than we knew it, and there were occasions when the men were too far from their home villages to go back at night. The van was still adequately provided for temporary accommodation, but, in our time, it was used as a store for the many spare parts; the big driving belts, oil and grease for the engine and, of course, our tea cups.

Sometimes, when it was really cold and he could safely leave the engine for a spell, Bill would take over from the one of us who looked nearest to freezing up and send her off to the van to "Look for the cap of the grease gun," or something equally unnecessary, and would offer the girl "five minutes to find it!" If it was anywhere near to break time, he would draw off a bucketful of hot water from the engine's boiler and send the most shivelled one to wash up the tea mugs. It was sheer heaven to get out of the cold and sit in the van's shelter for those few precious minutes, and we were very grateful for them and the many other kindnesses that helped us to get through that winter.

It was a source of amazement to us that the men did not seem to feel the extremes of weather. Neither of them wore overcoat, mac, hat or gloves, even when it was at its coldest, and they did not puff and sweat all over the place in the heat, which made their sympathy and help to us even more remarkable.

The heavy walking shoes issued to us were ideal for our work, and they were very comfortable to wear. They had just one drawback, and that only became obvious when we walked on concrete paving in the streets, or farmyards, especially if it happened to be frosty. The shoes were made from sturdy leather and, to add extra strength and lengthen their lives, a metal horse-shoe stud had been

built into the heels. Walking along a roadway or pavement, we sounded like a stampede of cavalry proportions and other pedestrians, hearing our approach from behind, were amazed upon looking around, to see that there were only the four of us. It was just impossible to walk quietly.

At times in the winter when the countryside was frozen solid or deep in snow, walking in those shoes was quite dangerous, and I cannot begin to record the number of times we did our own ungainly versions of 'The Skater's Waltz'! The most memorable and spectacular of these happened when we were going to catch a train from Tunbridge Wells. We came into the town on the first bus from the village to the bus terminus at the top of a steep hill. The railway station was situated at the bottom. With just five minutes or so to get from one to the other, we started to march downhill at a fair pace.

The pavement, deserted at that early hour, was still evenly coated with the heavy overnight frost, and we should have been more aware of this but were deep in enthusiastic discussion. It was not until I started to leave the group that the frost made itself noticeable. What began as a gentle slither gathered momentum on the steepness of the hill, until I was doing a slalom, arms flailing and body bent, in the frantic attempt to maintain my balance. The others girls were laughing, until they too came upon an extra slippery patch and joined the crazy, out of control glide to the station. There is no way adequately to describe the sheer absurdity of the spectacle, although when I saw the Disney film 'Fantasia' after the war, the dance of the hippos rang a loud bell! The real miracle was that none of us actually hit the deck, or suffered any injury — and we caught our train with minutes to spare!

Chapter 9

Spring, when it eventually arrived, made our struggles to survive the winter seem almost worthwhile — it was wonderful!

Mrs Bird's house stood on the corner of one of Bill's 'three went ways'. The main road which ran past the front of the house was bordered on the opposite side with the dense, neglected woods of a now derelict estate. At the bottom of a hill on our side was the smallholding of our nearest neighbour, and the other 'went' was a lane that ran along the side of the house, and that too was bordered with woodlands. This then was the perfect setting for us to experience our first ever natural spring. We watched the fat buds on the bare branches open into the daintiest new green leaves, until looking through the thickets was like peering through a fluffy mist. The ground beneath the trees became a carpet of colour, as bluebells, primroses, violets, wood anemones and many more of the wild spring flowers took their turns to produce a scenario that was so breathtakingly beautiful, we wanted to rush out and gather armfuls of it. From our bedroom windows we watched the antics of a squirrel family up in the branches of the trees that grew in the garden, and the rabbits, foraging near the edges of the woods, who became so used to our comings and goings that they ignored us most of the time.

As spring edged its way into summer, there were so many different things to discover among the multitude of birds nesting in the trees, we felt really ignorant, knowing so few of them. Sparrows and starlings ruled the roost in London, and there were so many more different varieties here. We had a very willing tutor in our landlady who, having lived all her life in the country, knew so much about the natural order of things and answered most of our questions about the birds and the woodland creatures.

Cycling to and from work, we saw lambs being born in the fields, calves on shaky legs huddling close beside their gentle mothers, and huge fat sows in their nursery sheds with clusters of tiny, squealing piglets milling around them in an everlasting struggle to gain access to the milk factory. Chicks, goslings and ducklings ran underfoot in the farmyards, and even the old farm tabby cats got into the act, with kittens in boxes in most barns. It was exciting, and very humbling, to realise the diversity of this spate of creation, how much we had missed in our education by living in a town. We were a regular bunch of softies over the wee animals and birds, suffering the derision of the locals as we grieved the loss of a runt piglet, tried to save a nestling fallen to the ground from its nest, or to succour a lost baby rabbit.

Everyone tried to explain that the runt pig rarely survives to do battle for its share of the food, that the birds that fall from nests or allow themselves to be pushed out, and the animals that get 'lost' are nature's rejects, that stand little chance of survival. But still we picked them up and carried them home, did all in our power to save them, and gave them a decent burial when, inevitably, they died.

We found it impossible to understand the attitudes of the country-bred folk, even our kind Mrs Bird, and many were the arguments we had on the rights and wrongs of trying to care for the least well endowed of wild things. How, for instance, we wondered, could a man who had so carefully and lovingly nurtured a litter of piglets, feeding them and keeping them warm, cheerfully see them loaded onto a lorry just a few months later, knowing that they were headed for a slaughterhouse or bacon factory? Or the poultry-man kill his charges with such obvious lack of concern? I am afraid we never stopped feeling that this callous attitude towards living creatures was one facet of the country-man's nature that would remain totally alien to us all the years we spent with them.

The arid heat of the summer that followed our first spring was almost as hard to cope with as the winter's cold. In the beginning, we were quite chuffed to see our skins acquiring such a healthy, golden glow, but as the hot, dry weather continued we began to resemble elongated coffee beans, which was neither so becoming, nor as comfortable. Our pasty-faced London friends, cooped up in their factories and offices, envied us the 'deep-roasted' look but we, on the whole, were far from enthusiastic about the process by which it was achieved. Even when the weather changed, and autumn was followed by another winter, our ruddy complexions only paled slightly and, with further roasting of successive summers to instil the tan even deeper, we had to come to terms with the permanent loss of our delicate, lily-white skins!

Chapter 10

Royalty and peers of the realm were not given to popping down to the East End for walk-abouts, it was not their scene, so obviously we had never had any sort of 'close encounter' with nobility, and had very confused ideas (gained mainly from the unreal world of the cinema) of what the upper crust was all about.

Because of this, it was with a great deal of curiosity that we approached the estate of a 'Real Live Lord'! The home farm of the estate had ploughed up grassland, and we had a stack of corn to thresh, the product of this patriotic sacrifice of paddock.

Bill said this Lord had some connection with the Ministry of Agriculture, and was particularly interested in our essay into the threshing scene — so, according to him, we had better be on our best behaviour, to give a good impression while we were there. Bert, as usual, made a joke of it, as he told us we must keep our hands clean at all times, just in case His Lordship felt like shaking them.

We did not mind what they said (used as we were by this time to getting our legs pulled): we were just consumed with curiosity! The house was quite the biggest we had ever seen, almost like a castle, and the gardens and home farm, in spite of wartime labour shortages, were absolutely immaculate!

The Estate Manager, an 'all-tweeds-and-pipe man', was quite friendly, in a 'posh' sort of way. He assured us that there would be no interference with our working system, and there was plenty of extra manpower, drawn from other sectors of the vast estate, to help everything to go with a swing.

At the first break he asked if we girls would 'volunteer' ourselves for collecting the tea from the house, and of course with the prospect of a closer look at the place we were more than willing! We were greeted by a haughty looking cook when we timidly knocked at the back door. She had the tea jug and tray of mugs at the ready for us and brought them to the door, quite clearly indicating that the doorstep was as near as four dirty urchins like us were likely to get to her spotless kitchen. We had to admit we agreed with her, it was a beautiful place, with gleaming copper pots hanging on hooks around the walls, shining black ranges, and a wooden table scrubbed almost white.

That kitchen must have been almost as big as the whole flat I was brought up in — and there was not a speck of dust, or a single thing out of place, in the expanse we could see from the doorway. A maid in all the proper gear (as seen at the cinema) was preparing vegetables at one of the sinks, and she was as neat (and as snooty) as Madam Cook.

We got on with the work quite well, everyone pulling their weight, and even the farmhands seemed to enjoy it. I suppose it was more of a novelty to them than most activities as the farm did not normally grow corn. Whenever the machine stopped, the estate chappie was about, talking to people, or just watching the procedures, and we wished all our farmers would take a leaf out of his 'non-interference' manual. It certainly made for better relations, and more efficient working, to be in such a friendly atmosphere.

We kept an eye open for sight of the lord, but saw no-one even remotely noble, although, as we freely admitted, we had no idea at all what we were looking for. Of course, we were not daft enough to expect him to turn out in his ermines, but we were very disappointed that he did not turn out at all!

On the second day, when we were nearing the end of the stack, Bill came up onto the top of the machine, where I was cutting bonds. "I'll take over for a minute," he said, holding his hand out for the knife, "His Lordship wants a word before we leave."

I was completely awestruck — the moment had finally come! I was about to meet and talk with a real live lord! Bill smiled at my expression, as I handed over the knife, "Go on!" he chuckled, "He's had his dinner already, so he won't be into eating you!" Stumbling eagerly down the ladder to ground level, I looked around. Everyone was working away as though nothing was amiss, I could not understand it at all. Had the lord got fed up with waiting for me to get down from the top? And then a cheerful voice from behind made me jump. "I'm glad you have a minute to spare,", His Lordship, the all-tweeds-and-pipe man said. "I've been agog to hear how you are coping with this job, and find I don't really need to ask. You are making a jolly good showing, I think!"

I honestly can't tell if I was relieved to find His Lordship not all that different from the next man, or disappointed that he WAS so ordinary! I do know I was horrified that I had been treating him with only the same degree of respect that I felt due to every farmer we worked for.

He seemed not to mind, or even to have noticed, our casual approach, and we were soon in deep discussion on things like working conditions, billeting arrangements and other things relevant to our situation. When he enquired about entertainment, he was staggered that we had been forbidden access to that offered to the troops by the W.V.S. and the N.A.A.F. No benefits or recreational facilities were open to us from these sources because we were 'not FIGHTING forces, only Land Girls''. Our lord thought this was a great shame, as (his words) we were doing such a cracking good job on the thresher, and we were away from our homes to do it, the same as the forces. He promised to put his mind to thinking up something to amuse us. It was with some regret that we packed up all the gear, and moved on. That beautiful place had been a bright spot in our normally down-to-earth slog.

I could not wait to get back to the billet to write home and boast, just a wee bit, about my actual meeting with a real live Lordship! Looking back on this encounter, I could see what a blessing it had been to be ignorant of His Lordship's identity (he was Lord Cornwallis) until the last minute. I was saved the dilemma of wondering how to address him — and — worst of all, whether I should do anything as out of the ordinary as to bow, or curtsey. I can imagine how utterly ridiculous either option would have been, performed by dusty urchins in dirty dungarees!

Chapter 11

Several weeks after this visit we received a surprise invitation. His Lordship, considering us as 'Cinderellas', had settled on the Merchant Navy as our counterparts in the 'beings overlooked' stakes, and he had arranged a dance in the village hall, to be attended by all available Land Army girls, and any Merchant Seamen at home on leave or waiting ship, with transport to be arranged for those outside of the village confines.

While we loved the idea of the dance, and really appreciated the kindness of its instigator, it brought to light a major deficiency in our wardrobes. Upon our admission into the service, we had forfeited our rights to civilian clothing coupons (which was only right and proper of course). We did still have our pre-war wardrobes at home, but what had not been taken into consideration was our growth rate. The open air life and manual work had filled out skinny factory worker bodies. We were broader across the back, and all the clambering about, and heaving of heavy objects, had given us sizable muscles to book. Nothing that we had worn before fitted anymore, even our shoes (those flimsy high heeled town specials) proving to be too narrow now. It seemed the only option, if we wanted to attend this dance at all, was to go in our uniforms, and, as we were all agreed that it would be most ungracious to the organiser if we did not show up, there followed an orgy of polishing and brushing up.

The Women's Land Army turned up in force like an army of tanks, and the expressions of the Merchant Seamen, at the sight of the 'baggy breeches brigade', were a picture! They, of course, still had civvy clothes that fitted them for time ashore, and they were quite smartly attired.

Everyone made an effort, and we were enjoying ourselves in spite of the 'fancy dress', until some of the local gentry, including His Lordship, turned up to share the treat, and give their support. The smart evening wear of the gentlemen, and the beautiful dresses of the ladies, made us all feel like ugly bugs, hulking great brutes among the elegant butterflies. From the moment of their arrival, our enjoyment of the dance went downhill at a gallop, and it was a relief when we could decently make our departure. To our group, the one bright spot in this 'infiltration' was His Lordship. He was a lovable man, and had obviously come to our evening with the intention of enjoying it. He singled out each one of our gang to dance with, and to announce to everyone in the vicinity, "This is one of MY gang," and really seemed to be proud of our achievements!

The dance was almost as much of a fiasco as our one, and only, dinner party. The squire and his wife invited us when we were doing the threshing on his land (I suspect it was a sort of let's do our bit for the war effort), but they were so very nice, we felt sure we would enjoy the dinner. Of course, we were faced with the same problem, what we HADN'T got to wear, but it seemed of less importance for an occasion like this than it had been for the dance.

We duly arrived at the large, imposing residence, and were cordially welcomed by our host and hostess. A rather prim maid struggled off with our heavy uniform coats, and we proceeded into the drawing room for pre-dinner drinks, before going into the dining room. The table was a truly wondrous sight, snowy white cloth, gleaming silver and glassware, and even a candelabrum thinga-mejig to add the final touch of elegance to the scene of opulence. We had never seen anything like it.

As we took our places, our hearts sank, for we noticed something that was bound to prove an embarrassment as the meal got under way. Life in a small flat with an overflowing family had never allowed for more than 'one of each' apiece, even had we been able to afford more than one course to a meal. This array of cutlery was a mystery of mammoth proportions to us of the rapidly sprouting chip-on-shoulder syndrome. We waded our way through five courses, each time waiting to see which implements our hosts picked up to use before we began to eat, and our glasses were re-filled with wine every time they were emptied. It was all so much richer in content than the plain food we were used to, and by the time the last course had been dealt with, we felt very full-heady from the wine, and slightly sick.

The squire and his lady had tried their utmost to find some common ground for conversation, but truly it was like the meeting of two different planets, with virtually no overlap between their life sheltered by wealth and social status, and our own hard working background. We all struggled to keep the chatter going, but it came as a relief to everyone when the Nanny came in to report that the children were now fast asleep, if we wished to visit the nursery (obviously considered to be the highspot of any evening). Trooping up the wide staircase and along a thickly carpeted corridor, behind the Nanny, we marvelled at the luxurious furnishings of bedrooms seen through open doors, and at the end of the corridor, two rooms for the children, a Day Nursery, and a Night one. They were lovely apartments for youngsters to grow up in, with bright pictures on the walls, great treasure chests of toys, a doll's house and a large spotted rocking horse.

The two children, little more than babes, were soundly sleeping in cots, with tinkling mobiles above, and it seemed a very peaceful place to end our visit. Nanny made it fairly plain to us that she resented the call to escort us round, for this whole set-up was beyond our ken, and she knew it! The politeness of all the servants we had been in contact with had been strained. It seemed to go against the grain with them to be serving the like of us on the same footing as their aristocratic employers. It was our first experience of this kind of inverted snobbery, but we came across it many times in our 'in between world' in the country.

Chapter 12

We always took sandwiches from our digs for our mid-day break, but it was the custom for farmers' wives to keep us supplied with tea. It was such a dusty job, the odd cuppa's helped us through the day, whatever the weather. A few farms offered an alternative, beer for the men mostly, but it was usually tea for us.

The strangest situation cropped up when we went for the first time to a fruit farm being run by a widower and his two single sons — no farmer's wife. All the men were working with the threshing, so with no one to make tea they brought out huge stone jugs of home-made cider before work started in the mornings and stood a box of cups and beakers with the jugs, in the shade away from the dust. Everyone was free to help themselves when they felt the need of a drink. The first day this happened it was a very welcome change to us girls. That cider was so cool and refreshing as it ran down our dry throats like liquid silk, and it WAS a very hot day.

"For goodness sake, go easy on the stuff," Bill cautioned, but, feeling extraordinarily fit and jolly, we pooh-poohed his warnings as we blithely went back for more. It was very odd that we did not feel the slightest bit tipsy until we got on our bikes at the end of the day for our four-mile ride home.

We tootled through the nearby village, Ellie and Dolly trying to harmonise one of the songs we had heard the evening before on Mrs Bird's wireless set, and even our reserved little Amy giggled to herself at some secret joke. Then we came to the hill. It was so exhilarating to feel the wind cooling our skin that we just let go, without a thought for the newly-learned 'heel-on-wheel' technique. The hill was a long steep gradient that carried on down for almost a mile, only levelling off just before a sharp bend to the right.

We had never been that way before, as we had come to the farm with the thresher from another direction, so of course we had no idea at all what might be lying in wait for us hidden around that bend. We met it going full out, with all the impetus of the long hill behind us, swooped round it in our 'all-over-the-road' formation

— and ran slap into a railway crossing gate which just happened to be closed for the 'train of the day'! We made something of a mess, with our poor old bikes coming off marginally worse than their decidedly tipsy riders. As we hobbled the last three miles back to Mrs Bird's, pushing our badly buckled bikes, we mentally signed the pledge. All further visits to that particular farm were supplemented with water-bottles.

I think it was this incident that finally tipped the balance for Amy. She was not happy with our job. The noise and bustle of the machine got on her nerves and she loathed being so dirty all the time. Naturally shy and reserved with strangers, she did not like the constant moving from farm to farm, never being able to get to know people enough to let down the barriers. She really had tried to adjust, but I think smashing up the bikes and having to walk so far to get home finally convinced her that this work was not for her.

Amy got her transfer fairly quickly, for a person really had to like the work to be any way good at it in our job. We were sorry to see her go, of course, but we were happy for her too, especially when we later heard that she was in her seventh heaven, living in the farmhouse of an elderly farmer and his wife (who were totally spoiling her, by the sound of it) and learning to look after their small herd of dairy cows. This, we felt sure, was much more our Amy's cup of tea than threshing. The replacement for Amy soon arrived — or rather, she did not actually need to 'arrive' since she was already there.

Di was a local girl who lived in the village and had had the same sentiments as ours when her time came for conscription; she did not have any yen to go into the armed forces. Di was a regular laugh-a-minute from the first day, and her teasing take-offs of our cockney oddities became catch-phrases, to be thrown back at us whenever appropriate by Bill and Bert and the farmhands.

"It aint arf rainin in it" and "Blimey, its ot" were bandied about willy nilly, but we did not mind, it was not nastily meant, and we had not realised how strange some of our sayings sounded to these country people. And we had laughed at their 'wents'.

Di was a lovely looking girl, with rosy cheeks and naturally curly hair that was the envy of us all, especially when, in the rain, ours would be hanging like rats tails. She just could not help herself when it came to flirting, and there was not a single man in the

district who had not at some time wanted to date her. I am not only talking of the farmhands either, our Di had half the personnel from the army camp nearby on her trail too!

She fitted in well with the rest of the gang, and was very welcome, as we had all been missing Amy. Living in her parents' home as she did, she had lots more time (and spare cash) for going out with her various boyfriends, and kept us in touch with quite hilarious graphic descriptions of her exploits.

Our Sundays were so full of necessary chores, hair-washing, laundry, room-cleaning and, of course, writing letters, that we had little time or energy for any sort of commitment. Ellie was the only one with a serious attachment, being engaged to a Sapper, who was at that time up in Scotland training for overseas posting. He and Ellie devised a system for keeping in touch by public telephone. Frank, the soldier, could get away from the camp by eight o'clock in the evening, unless he had a guard duty, and there was a phone box near to the gates. Ellie, Dolly and I would bike down to our village just before eight, and wait outside the box for the phone to ring. Then, while Ellie and Frank had their three minutes together (albeit in phone boxes hundreds of miles apart) Dolly and I would race twigs from the bridge of the little stream that ran through the village High Street. It became such a regular occurrence that we were all bereft when Frank, his training complete, was posted overseas. The 'phone-run' ended, and Ellie had to revert to letter-writing.

Chapter 13

Farmers' reactions to girls on the circuit were mixed, especially in the beginning when we were such an unknown quantity. Threshing really had never been considered a suitable job for women, although many of the farm women we met seemed to be expected to do lots of things we considered more unpleasant.

Before the war there had been no problem, for the farmers could usually find the odd gipsy men and other 'travellers', not fussy what they did, and glad of a few days on 'casual'. Threshing times were not popular with the regular farmhands, since it upset their routine of normal working. The job being continuous once the machine started, there were not the usual short stops to take a breather, have a chat or, perhaps, a few puffs on pipe or cigarette. So we were never welcomed with open arms by the resident work-force and, if the farmer himself happened to be anti, we really needed the clan feeling that was growing strongly between our two B's and the gang.

After our initial visit to his farm, a farmer was usually favourably impressed by 'them women' and we quite enjoyed working for them as a rule. There had to be one exception, and ours was a thick-set, bull-necked little man with a red, apoplectic-looking complexion and very small, angry eyes. Known by all and sundry as 'Piggy', I think he hated all of the human race, but most of all he loathed women.

My job, as the forewoman of the gang, involved reporting to the farmer upon our arrival at his farm to see if there were any variations in the way he wanted the work done and finding out if we needed to go to the farmhouse to collect the tea at the breaks, or were having it brought out by the wife. Most of our farmers took this opportunity before the hustle and bustle began to have a chat: the progress of the war, his particular difficulties (they all had some) and general gossip. Mr Piggy was not like that. He would never waste a word where a grunt would fit the bill, his orders being terse to the point of rudeness, with each word spat out like an offending fruit pip. The only time in my whole life that I took part in militant action, this horrible man was the cause.

We had been on the circuit for almost a year when it happened, and we were by that time extremely competent at our job, well versed in the ways of the different farms and farmers, and we felt we were, at the very least, respected by them all. Our visit to 'Piggy's' farm on this occasion started in the same vein as usual, with him snapping and grunting and everyone doing their best to ignore his rudeness. This time, however, he was not going to be satisfied with having the cavel raked back out of the way, but had thought up a real beauty of a complication for us.

There was a shed about a hundred yards from the scene of operations, and he wanted the cavel in that. His idea was that the girl with the rake should load as much as possible onto a huge sheet of sackcloth, pick it up by the corners, lug it to the shed and tip it off the cloth into the shed. I tried to tell the man the facts of life in the cavel game. The stuff churned out of the machine so quickly, and in such large amounts, that all this raking onto cloths, lugging and tipping out just was not feasible. He seemed to take a positively malicious pleasure, however, in his insistence that this was how he wanted it done and that was how we'd B-well do it! So we had to give it a go.

It was not very long before the shed was so full that the girl on cavelling had to stop after tipping each fresh load in, to trample it down and make another few inches of space for the next batch. This took so much time — and the old machine just kept churning it out — that the heap under the thresher rose until, having jammed into a tight wedge between the ground and the machine, it spilt out and started to pile up on all sides of it. When it began to interfere with the interior workings, the drive wheel jammed and threw the big main belt off. End of operations!

Bill and Bert were furious! They would now have to delve deep to find what damage had been caused, and if the machine would work again. But their anger was as a feather in the wind compared with the wrath of Mr Piggy. Face purple, eyes bulging, he turned the whole of his malice onto the cavel girl, who happened to be Di, and flayed her with a tirade of abuse. Amidst the worst of the cursing, the more printable (if no less acceptable) included references to "Lazy cows" and "Bloody idle no-good women". When he finally ran out of steam, he looked around at the farm men who were

standing open-mouthed at such vicious verbals, and then, with a
nasty smirk, Mr Piggy really cooked his goose with this parting
shot: "The lazy bitches will be holding out their hands for tips
when they finish. Well! I can tell you now, they'll get nothing but
good riddance from me!"

We had had more than enough. Poor Di (who really had been
trying her damnedest to cope with the cavel) was nearly in tears,
and the others were white as sheets after the stream of invective.
His remark about the tip was the final straw. We never expected
tips (or got any) on any of the farms, although we did gladly accept
any fruit that was going to waste. I looked around at the white
faces, and something exploded inside me: "Come on, girls," I
called, "War or no war, we don't have to put up with this filth!"
and we started walking towards the hedge where our bikes were
leaning.

The farm hands were flabbergasted. No one, it seemed, had ever
tried to stand up to the beastly man before. It took a few seconds

before it filtered through to Mr Piggy that a large portion of his workforce was walking away from the job, and, when it did, he came very near to exploding. With more obscenities pouring from his vile mouth, he started after us, and I think he would have laid into us with his fists if Bill had not intervened. Stepping calmly into the raging man's path, he started to utter a few quiet words that no one but Mr Piggy could hear. We never discovered what was said, for Bill would never tell us, but whatever it was, it worked a miracle.

With a visible effort at self control, the horror stood for a moment, then walked over to where we stood by the hedge. He asked me to reconsider my decision, saying he could not find other labour to run the machine if we left, and he would go broke if he did not get his corn done. It was not anything like an apology of course, but I think that was as near to making one as he had ever been forced to go. It was obvious to everyone how much it was hurting him to be speaking civilly to anyone! He sent for tea, and got everyone going on the awful job of clearing the huge accumulation of cavel away from the machine. It took Bert half an hour to find and repair the damage, and only then were we operational again. There was no mention of cloths, and sheds, and the cavel was raked back into a pile out of the way as we always did it.

We went back to that farm many times over the years, and Mr Piggy stayed clear, never coming near us girls, nor making any attempt to alter work patterns. He never — ever — spoke to any one of us again.

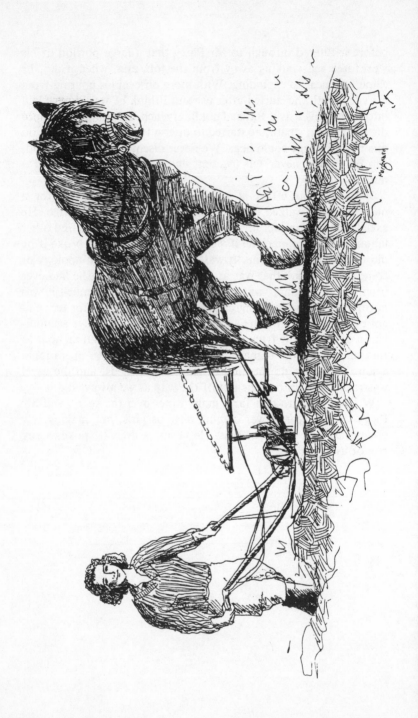

Chapter 14

Threshing operations began as soon as the harvesting was over, round about the end of August – beginning of September, and they would carry on right through the winter until every stack of corn in the area had been dealt with, which was usually sometime in May.

When it was all done, Bill would depart with his steam engine to do other forms of traction work for the summer. Bert went back to the yard with the machines, and spent the 'idle' months cleaning, repairing and repainting the battered old things, to help them last out for another year's grind. As for us, we were hired out to any farmer desperate enough to take his chances with four absolute greenhorns in all aspects of farming except threshing! It seemed very strange, and often boring, to be working in one place for so long, and we would soon be itching to be on the move again. The work was totally different, and each summer we learned new skills.

On our first farm we had been hoeing for days, finding it extremely boring. Then one morning the farmer came into the field in a state of annoyance, as his carter had gone sick halfway through harrowing a field. They were waiting to plant, and there was no other experienced person to carry on the job, so he was faced with asking one of us. I clicked for the job, mainly because all the others chickened out, and off I went with the farmer to the half-harrowed field. Here I was introduced to Bob, who was patiently chewing his way through the hedge near the gate.

He was a very large specimen, as horses go, broad in the beam and with white feathery hair surrounding his great hooves.

"You don't need to worry too much about leading the old devil," the farmer laughed, smacking the nearest haunch affectionately. "He's done this job so many times, he knows it better'n anyone! — one thing, though — hang on to him when you get to the ends nearest to the yard, he's always hoping it's time to go back to his stable at that point!" And then, by way of an after thought as he turned to leave, he called over his shoulder, "And watch out for his feet when you have to turn round!"

This last seemed rather cryptic at the time, but when I reached the end of that first row, I got his meaning. I think Bob released all his frustrations at the long straight pull up the row when he reached the end and it was turn around time. I also feel sure that he knew exactly what he was doing when his great feet flipped around all over the place until one of them located mine, and he attempted to stand on my toes! This playful frolic brightened his day, that was obvious, but I was very relieved that his sense of direction was defective. I am no judge of horse weight, but it was easy to see that one of those feet could have made mincemeat of one of mine. During the next few hours I became a dab hand at dodging when we came to the turning points and, on the whole, I think we both enjoyed our day. My constant chattering must have been a change for him from the sparse conversation of the carter (who was rather grim), while the novelty of being so close to this lovely animal was really satisfying to me.

The other girls thought I must have been bored out of my mind, being on my own all day, but when I told them how enjoyable it had been they rather hoped that the carter's sick spell would last a few more days so that they could have a turn with Bob. Sadly, the malady was a brief affair, and Bob lost his chatterbox companion the next day.

I told my mother about him, thinking it would make her laugh, but she was horrified. Being totally ignorant of threshing, she had taken my word for it that it was, so to speak, a piece of cake, and of course I had always played down the rigours of our early months. But a horse she knew about! There were lots of them in London, delivering goods. She knew how big they were, and only remembered how weak I had been before the weathering and hardening up of the 'weed'!

Chapter 15

One summer we were hired out to the big estate on the opposite side of the road to Mrs Bird's. We had to ride along an overgrown driveway to get to the farm section of the estate, and we really loved that part of the ride. Right in the middle of the woodlands we came upon the ruins of Scotney Castle, with a weedy moat surrounding it and straggling Rhododendrons everywhere. In the early morning mist it looked very mysterious, and we always paused when we reached it to fantasise on how it must have looked in its prime.

The farm, on the other side of the woodland, was very extensive, almost reaching the outskirts of three surrounding villages, and we had been hired as 'sheepdogs'! Our main occupations were the bringing in of flocks of sheep, and taking them back again. They needed this shunting around for the shepherds to dock the lambs' tails and dose up the ewes. That sounds fairly straightforward I know, but the enormous extent of the farm territory did create a few problems.

Upon our arrival each morning, the head shepherd would designate which of the flocks he wished to treat on that day, and in what order he wanted them brought in. Then we would cycle to the first field, which could be anything up to two miles distant from the treatment sheds, round up the resident ewes and lambs, and drive them to the farm, where the shepherds would be waiting with tail-docking implements and bottles of medication.

As there were usually in excess of one hundred ewes, and at least as many lambs, this driving was no walk-over, and we must have been quite a strange sight, had there been anyone to see it, cycling round and round the silly beasts endeavouring to achieve some sort of order, and get them onto the road. Even then we could still be in trouble, as a lamb would find any small gap in the fence or hedge to wriggle through. Its frantic mother would start to panic the rest, and before we knew what was happening the lot already out on the road would begin to stampede — and we would still have the wretched escapee lamb to catch!

Once having got them safely to the farm, we had to turn them out in a small paddock, and then the really tricky business began. Called separation, it involved mixing ourselves in with the swirling mass of agitated sheep, catching one ewe and her lamb, or lambs, and taking them in opposite directions, the ewe to one end of the barn to be dosed from a bottle, and her offspring to another shepherd who was taking the messy ends from their tails.

It is impossible to describe the confusion involved in sorting one family group from the milling mass of woolly coats, and, having achieved that, the removal of the lambs from mothers. The lambs would yell and the ewes would fight us — we had no idea that sheep could be so aggressive.

After each family had been attended to, we let them out into a larger paddock at the back of the barn where there was more din as mothers bleated to find their infants, and lambs yelled both for their mums and for their sore tails. The hours spent in the heat of so much fleece, and the din of so many unhappy sheep, left us drained, and it was a relief when, the flock all treated, we had to round them up and start the long trek back to their field. Meanwhile the shepherds cleaned up the debris and prepared new batches of medicine ready for the next lot. We would all breathe a sigh of relief as the latch on the field gate clicked into place behind the last stragglers, and we could take a minute or two to regain our cool before proceeding to the next field on our list, and starting the rigmarole over again.

Strangely enough, although it may not sound like it, we did enjoy the experience, for it was far more interesting than the interminable hoeing and weeding that we sometimes had to do. On our way to work one morning we had quite an adventure to brighten things up for us. We had paused, as we usually did, to lean on our bikes and gaze across the moat to the 'Fairytale castle'. The mist was rising from the stagnant water, and the ruin looked eerie, with its tangled skirt of over-grown bushes — we had named it 'Sleeping Beauty's Hide-away'. Ellie raised her nose in the air and sniffed, then with a look of total disbelief she sniffed again. "Our sleeping beauty must have woken up hungry!" she said, "She's cooking herself breakfast — and it's BACON!" We thought perhaps it was the strange atmosphere surrounding the old place causing hallucinations until, one by one, our noses caught the aroma too. Someone, not so far away, was frying bacon!

No big deal these days of course, but in wartime Britain bacon was so scarce that if and when people were able to get some, they would treat it like the proverbial gold dust, using it in a pie or a pudding to make it stretch further.

This tantalizing smell wafting through the trees was just about the most extravagantly delicious scent we had ever been privileged to sniff. We just had to follow our noses, an occurrence of this magnitude had to be investigated, even if it made us late for work. We located the source about fifty yards from the castle, and I do not know who was most surprised, the group of soldiers sitting round a fry-pan cooking breakfast, or the four drooling appetites that burst through the undergrowth. They were doing some sort of jungle preparation, they told us, finding it infinitely boring, and would we like to join them for breakfast? There were fat juicy sausages sizzling in the pan beside the bacon — how could we resist?

That was the most delicious of breakfasts, our second of that morning I am ashamed to say, but we were made very welcome to share it. I think the soldiers enjoyed having someone different to talk to, and those woods resounded with their laughter as we told them of our function as sheepdogs, and the other odd jobs we had done. As we reluctantly took our leave, they invited us to 'Follow our noses' again any time we happened to be in the locality. They were about in the woods for several days, and we managed to sniff them out on three more of them. It really was a miracle that we could still do our work with any degree of efficiency after those luxury second breakfasts.

A rather amusing incident also connected with sheep happened on another of our summer hirings. On this occasion we were sent to a mixed farm consisting of some sheep, a few pigs, a couple of cows and two hop-gardens, but the main product was fruit, of which there was a wide variety.

We were quite pleased when we were told that our first job would be plum picking, thinking it would be a doddle. To get to the plum orchard in a direct line meant crossing two fields, and we set off gaily on our first morning, carrying deep baskets that could be hooked onto ladder rungs, and a healthy appetite for plums! Half-way across the first field we met the old shepherd. "Don't you young gels be daring to cross that field with my ewes in," he warned, "They do be troublesome one's, and I don't want they scaried, so you'd best to walk round."

The detour we had to make to avoid the sheep field was through a tangly copse, and along a path overgrown with nettles, and we did NOT think a lot of that. During the course of the long day that followed, we discovered that standing on the narrow rungs of the ladders for extensive periods was crippling on the feet. We discovered that although the fruit seemed to hang up there waiting to be picked so easily, when we climbed the ladder we had invariably set it up in the wrong position, and most of the fruit that had looked so close from the ground would be just out of reach, and down the wretched ladder we would have to go, to move it round the tree a bit.

We found that wasps were even more partial to nice juicy plums than we were, and that they ate their way into the fruit headfirst. When an incautious hand closed around a wasp-inhabited plum, it also closed on the wasp's posterior, where the sting is. But, greatest of all these drawbacks, we experienced the acute discomfort brought on by eating too much of the farmer's profit!

At the end of the day we just could not face going all that long way round to avoid a few sheep, thinking that surely, if we were very quiet and unobtrusive, the silly animals would not even notice our passage through their territory.

We came to the gate, which was fastened with a huge padlock, but quite climbable, dumped our bags and picking baskets over, and were about to follow them into the field when the farm foreman, on his way to the farm, stopped to tell us that we had done a pretty good job with the plum-picking. He warned us "Don't let old Perce see you crossing his field — he's real panicking over his old ewes."

We bade him Goodnight, climbed over the gate, and reached for our bags and baskets. Something was amiss; there were four of us, and we had each thrown a bag and a basket into the field, where now there were certainly four bags, but only three baskets!

A rumble from Ellie turned gradually into hysterical laughter, as she pointed across the grass. Running round in circles, and vigorously shaking her head, was one of Perce's pets wearing the very latest thing in headgear, a plum basket. The smell of plums still lingering in it must have lured her into poking her head in to find the source, and it had wedged firmly, with the rigid wicker handle encircling her neck, tight enough to stop the silly thing pulling her head out again.

Well! Scary or not, that ewe was well and truly chased around the field, as we tried to catch it and relieve it of its unusual headgear. All the others, not recognising it as a fellow creature in its strange bonnet, got in a panic too, which added considerably to the general confusion. It took us over twenty minutes to catch the daft creature, and another three or four to wrestle her into submission to wriggle the basket over her head, and give her back the gift of sight. The ewe was not as grateful for our exertions on her behalf as she might have been. In fact the whole flock of about fifty fat old things retreated at great speed to the far corner of the field.

The next day, as we started across the first field, we met old Perce the shepherd again. "It's all right for you to go across that field if you wants to," he told us, "There baint no ewes out there now, I've had to move 'em all up into the lambing pens, cause they

72

decided to start in the night." His old eyes twinkled somewhat, as with a wry grin he added, "Had proper trouble with them — late lambing — thought they'd be still-borns I did — but something made 'em liven their ideas up last night! — it's done 'em a power of good. They all dropped them O.K. — and they're all live twins!"

As we passed through the now open gate, and into the second field, the old chap called "Have you a good plumming my lassies — and mind you don't get dropping them baskets all over the place!"

Chapter 16

When we were on the move from farm to farm, we found right from the first what a disadvantage it was to be female! Farmers' wives were usually most generous with supplies of tea throughout the day, for which we were, of course, very grateful, but that, as far as they were concerned, was the full limit of their co-operation on a woman to woman basis.

Not once at any of the farms were we offered the use of the facilities of the farmhouse. Being unable to wash dirty hands before eating our sandwiches was not too insurmountable a problem, for we could leave a small part still wrapped as a handle, but there was no easy answer to the question of going to the toilet. Our first action, therefore, upon reaching a new site of operations, had to be a scout round for a suitable cover point in readiness for our hasty dive when the machine shut down for dinner-break. An old shed, a clump of bushes, or even a deep ditch, were the best we could hope for. The menfolk never had this problem; a quick nip round to the blind side of the stack, or behind a tree, was ample opportunity for them, but for us girls with overall coats to remove before dungarees could be unhitched, it was a constant source of embarrassment.

Sometimes the stack we were working had been built away from farm buildings, out in the open with no available cover, and on these occasions we would have to ask Bill's help. He was always very understanding of our difficulty in these matters and when things were just too awkward for us to cope, he would ask those men not going home for their dinner break to sit on one side only of the thresher, instead of spreading themselves around to eat their food. This at least gave us the shelter of the mounds of cavel on the other side. It was really very fortunate that we had such good control over these natural functions, as in most cases the break at mid-day offered the only opportunity for us to go.

It was never a 'comfortable' situation, especially when the weather was very cold, or when it snowed, and we felt ourselves lucky that we escaped the humiliation of frost-bite in the 'Nether-lands'! For all this awkwardness, we could understand the unwill-ingness of the wives to have us go into their homes. No housewife worthy of her salt would willingly countenance having a herd of straw and dust spreaders passing through a clean house, and the thought of the ensuing mess must have allayed any pangs of con-science they might have felt about our having to forage round for ourselves.

Our most embarrassing of all moments occurred on the occasion of our second assignment with nobility, a Lady this time. Long before our visit to her farm, we had been getting the message loud and clear from both Bill and Bert that this one might carry a title, but she "Warn't no real Lady, NO WAY!"

It took much patient digging to get the complete story (as they knew it of course, and there was no guarantee that it was the truth). According to the men, the old Lord, of authentic, bluer-than-blue blood, had no heir or kin of any kind to inherit the title and his considerable wealth. What he did have was a middle-aged secretary who had served him faithfully through most of her working life. Knowing that, when he died, she would have difficulties in settling down into another job, even if she could get one, he asked her to marry him. It was not very long after this marriage of convenience (and respect) that he died and she, of course, inherited the lot. We thought it was a lovely story and, when it was time to go to her estate for threshing, and we met her, we felt that she was more deserving of her title than a lot who were born into the nobility.

It was a strange facet of the country people's outlook that a Lord or a Lady had to be conceived 'properly' in the master bedroom, and they seemed to feel they could only give respect to the ones who ate their jam from the traditional silver plate.

The widow, who for anonymity's sake I will call Lady Florence, was a thick set horsey woman who seemed to live perpetually in tweeds and jodhpurs, and this was no surprise as she had a string of the most handsome thorough-breds in the extensive stables. She had a hearty but by no means bossy way of talking to people, which was probably the reason for the antipathy, noticeable mostly among the men. Women bosses were not as prevalent in those days of un-equal opportunities for us females, and I guess the men felt a trifle emasculated in having to take orders from her.

We were going to thresh fodder beans, a crop several in her position went for when they ploughed up previously uncultivated grassland. Beans, although a useful crop, did not need a great deal of specialised knowledge. Lady Flo had sacrificed two paddocks of grazing and produced a large stack of beans, which we were going to put through the thresher. The sieves on the machine had to be bigger for beans than those used for corn, and Bert needed to alter the alignment in the drum as well, so while he attended to that, and Bill got steam up in the engine, we took the opportunity to investigate the out-buildings, and find the best location for our mid-day 'dash'.

We found the ideal place in the long row of stables. One stall that had obviously been free of horses for some time had the entire front half nearest to the door piled up with hay, but when we clambered over this to the rear, we found a clear space, with concrete floor and a drain. We felt quite pleased with our find, knowing how well we could conceal ourselves behind the huge heap of hay.

We found Lady Flo extremely amenable to work for. She listened to our suggestions and, conceding that we knew more about the threshing scene, let us get on with the job with no interference at all. She was generous with tea, sending one of the servants (I think he was the chauffeur) with an enormous teapot full to the brim with a nice strong brew, a jug that held at least a gallon of milk, and a large bowl of precious rationed sugar. On another tray with mugs for the tea was a basket arrangement of dry biscuits. There was ample for everyone to have a handful of biscuits, and a second mug of tea. That was the mid-morning break, but we 'hadn't seen nothing yet' (as they say in all the old movies). We found her generosity overwhelming when the machine stopped for lunch. After the extra mugfuls of tea we had drunk earlier, we really needed to dash off straight away, but the good lady was there before we had even reached the ground, and everyone was herded round to the front of the house.

We could not believe our eyes when we saw, on the patio a long trestle table, positively groaning under the weight of the fodder piled upon its length. There were hot individual pies, bread rolls, great hunks of cheese, salad stuff, pickles, more of the dry biscuits and, to round off (IF anyone had any space left) little apple pies. Standing on a smaller table was all the tea paraphernalia and, in addition, bottled beer for those who preferred it. It really was a feast, and we cheerfully postponed our visit to the stable in honour of all that lovely food, making sure we ate our full share of it too!

In consequence of this piggish obsession with non-stop eating, we did not get away to the stables until there were only five minutes to starting up time. Locating our stable, we dashed over the pile of hay, relieved the tension satisfactorily — and it was then that calamity overtook us. He was just a man with a barrow actually, but to us in our embarrassing position, he was BIG TROUBLE. Quite leisurely he began to fork loads of the hay onto the barrow, whistling softly to himself, and it was obvious there was no one timing him.

We heard Bill start the threshing machine, and knew we should be out there, waiting to begin work, but we could do nothing but stay crouched behind the hay. To adjust our clothing we must needs stand up, and to stand up would be to expose ourselves. What a fix to find ourselves in! Eventually, his barrow piled high, the man pushed it through the stable door. Oh, what a relief — But then we heard him stop, turn, and lock the door behind him. Now what were we going to do?

Hastily we sorted ourselves out, then hunted around in the hope that there would be another door somewhere, perhaps one connecting with the other stables. No such luck: we were well and truly caught. We banged on the door, and shouted ourselves hoarse, but the steam engine was puffing out its fresh boost up, and the threshing machine had now started, which was always a guaranteed deafener. No one could hear our now frantic pleas to be let out. Bill blew a loud blast on the whistle. We knew he must be really mad with us, we were already five minutes late, and everyone would be hanging about waiting to start, as they could not do without us in position.

Eventually, a Bill we did not often see (really angry) came looking for us, and found us locked in the stables. It was a very sheepish quartet that followed him back to the threshing, to the catcalls and crude remarks of the hands. There just had to be some wag who would remember the old rhyme about the old ladies locked in the lavatory. We were not all that bothered about them, for we would be on our way from this farm after two days, but it did worry us that we had caused Bill to get so angry, and it was a great relief when he eventually simmered down and began to see the funny side of it.

We had quite a few laughs to make the days brighter, but just occasionally we came upon a bit of a joker who was not all that funny, and such a one was Ben. Apart from people with special jobs (cowmen, shepherds and such), the farm workers fell mainly into two groups, the elders, too old to be called up, and youngsters, not yet old enough. Ben was among this category, about sixteen we thought. Most of the lads, though a trifle slap-dash in their approach to work, were fine to get on with, but this Ben was a JOKER. We endured an almost non-stop stream of inane witticisms, and in addition he made a speciality of practical jokes. We did not know how the older men, who had to put up with him all the time, kept their sanity. On our second day at that farm we were trying to get the stack finished in time to pack up and move on to the next farm while the daylight lasted. It was too tricky a business getting our cavalcade along the lanes in the dark.

Everyone put their backs into it — except Ben, and the jokes came fast and furious from that lad. Tools put aside for a moment disappeared, and time would be wasted hunting for them. One poor old soul found a dead rat in his lunchbag when we stopped for tea, and when he had finished break and went back to start work, an armful of thistles had mysteriously deposited themselves in Bert's 'standing hole' on the machine. It was so silly, we felt like whopping the fool. At last, in spite of the hindrances, we did finish in time and, while we were helping with the packing up, one of the older men chided Ben on his stupid games.

"Ah," said Ben, "But I did make April Fools of everyone, didn't I?"

The farmer, who was nearby signing Bill's chit for the threshing hours, looked up.

"Don't be dafter than you have to, Ben!" he called, "YESTERDAY was April Fools Day — not today."

Suddenly, I felt very sad. I could understand how, with all the traumas of the war, others had forgotten the date, but what seemed so awful was the fact that I had forgotten too. April First was my birthday, and in 1941 a very special one. I had gone and worked right through my twenty-first birthday, my 'coming of age', without even knowing it. That surely made me the biggest April Fool of all time!

Chapter 17

We always found the children on farms rather daunting, whether they were the farmer's own or the offspring of the workforce. They were so different from the noisy extrovert London kids we knew. I suppose that was understandable, really.

Where we came from, overcrowding was the norm and our mothers were glad to get the youngsters out from underfoot by letting them play in the street. Streets were not dangerous places for them then, the few delivery vans that traversed them being slow, horse-drawn vehicles that could be heard approaching long before they passed. Rich people, the only ones who could afford the new-fangled motor cars, had no cause or wish to come to the East End. So it was that from a very early age there would always be lots of others to play with, to sit on the kerb and tell stories to, or to do battle with. Necessity taught us young Londoners to be brash, noisy and well able to stand up for what few rights we had.

Children on farms had very different beginnings. Often family units would be isolated from others by sheer distance, until the children reached school age, and they were, on the whole, much quieter and more self-contained. We found it unnatural that they could stand and watch us working for quite long periods without uttering a word, whereas a London child would not have been able to resist chattering nonstop, even if it were only nonsense.

Some of the farmers' children, especially on the more prosperous farms, were supercilious little brats, even the quite young ones. I remember on one such farm the son, aged about four, asked his mother within our hearing, "What are those awful dirty people doing in OUR farmyard Mummy?" We expected 'Mummy' to scold his rudeness, but to our horror she was equally bad-mannered when she told him "We have to have them to do the work, darling, but they'll only be here a few days, I promise."

We may not ever be rich or well educated, we thought, but if a child of ours were only half as rude as that one, he would have 'something to get on with' (as my mother always said when she gave us a wallop where it hurt most!).

Luckily we did not have too much contact with children of that ilk. Most farm labourers' broods were not at all insolent, just very very quiet. When we looked back to our first 'close encounter', the time we had almost mowed down about a dozen of them, we recalled something that had not registered at the time. We had not known those youngsters were just around the bend as we approached it, because they were not making any noise. They had been walking up that road in silence, twelve children — silent! They had walked round us as we were heaped on the road without uttering a word, and their progress after they passed us remained singularly quiet.

The thing we found most off-putting was the children's scorn when we showed any nervousness in dealings with livestock. One farm we visited had a cornstack built two fields away from the farm yard, and it could only be reached by crossing the intervening field which contained a herd of cattle. We had got quite used to cows by this time, but these beasts in the field were not cows, they were young bullocks being fattened up to be beef one day. Bullocks can be rather scary as they are very unpredictable creatures. For no apparent reason one will start to gallop off, and before you can blink the whole kit and caboodle will constitute a carefree stampede. Or, being curious animals, they will start to follow anyone crossing their terrain, and by sheer weight of numbers, with those at the rear pushing to get a good look, will before long be right on the heels of the walkers.

We were always apprehensive while crossing this field, and it must have showed. On our third and last day at the farm we found young James, aged no more than six, waiting at the gate into the field when we arrived. Without a word, he opened the gate for us to pass through, then went on ahead, herding the cattle away from us to the other side. His look of derision as he held the opposite gate for us to leave the field made us feel about two feet tall!

We had a similar experience with a flock of geese one day on another farm. We had been given the freedom of an orchard full of plum-laden trees which the farmer had been unable to get picked in time. To reach this orchard we had to walk over a small bridge across a stream and this was quite straightforward when in our dinner break we wandered over to the fruit trees to pick our own dessert. When we started back, however, there was a flock of geese well established and grazing on the approach to the bridge.

We had met geese before, and always managed not to get too close to them but to cross that bridge we would have to pass right through the flock. We had often been told by farm people that geese were no problem if you just ignored them, so, gathering up our courage, we marched in tight formation right through their ranks, trying to kid ourselves that they were not there. But they were — and they did not like us walking among them as if we had every right to. They started to demonstrate this disapproval in no uncertain terms, for as we reached the bridge, two huge ganders began nipping at our heels. Panic to the fore, we started to run. This seemed to be the signal for all the rest of the wretched creatures to join in, and we were absolutely terrified as the whole lot of them, long necks stretched and wings beating the air, squawked in our wake.

Quite suddenly the din eased off, and then stopped altogether. When we finally plucked up enough courage to look behind us, Mary and Jenny, the cowman's twins, were calmly herding the geese back across the bridge. What really hurt was the reproach on their faces as they came back, and Mary remarked, in a very accusing tone, "Grown-up people ought to know better than to go around frightening poor dumb animals."

Chapter 18

Doing our laundry at the 'Suet' house had been an agony of confidence-breaking proportions. We had never had to wash our own clothes before, and ours were always so very dirty. The water came from a large rain-water butt and we were rationed to one bucketful a wash. Our toilet soaps were not a great success in cold water but, in a way, this was a benefit, as one bucketful of rinsing water among four of us would not have coped with a vast amount of lather.

As our 'cleans' were not a lot different from the 'dirty' state (apart from being very wet) we were allocated a small, well hidden line behind a shed. Inadequate in length, and unblown by even the slightest breeze, the clothes turned out looking worse on Mondays, after washdays, than they had on Saturday, at the end of a week's dusty threshing. Sunday morning washing sessions at Mrs Bird's house were totally different — it was fun there.

My Mum spent most of her day on Mondays with the weekly family wash, hours bent over the sink scrubbing away at the clothes with a large cake of coarse Sunlight soap and a washboard, before the end product of her toil could be seen, flapping in the wind from the complex of lines that criss-crossed the yard. With a factory that specialised in cleaning used sacks backing onto the yard, the 'lovely lines of whites' that she took such pride in soon took on the hue of whatever produce had been in the sacks currently going through the cleaning process in the factory. When the wind was blowing our way, the 'clean' washing often picked up the smells too, so it was not unusual to have a strong aroma of spices, pepper or some other unidentifiable, but equally pungent, nose twitcher for the first day of clean clothes.

Mrs Bird's clothes line was fastened between two sturdy trees and, once loaded, could be hoisted up high into the air, with forked branches trimmed to make props. The cobbled yard sloped very slightly towards the centre, where there was a drain next to the pump. One of the outbuildings was a washhouse, with a copper for boiling, a deep sink (no taps of course) and wooden slatted racks for hanging things to drip-dry on when the weather was bad. There was a gully running through the length of the washhouse to the drain to deal with the drips from wet washing hung in there.

We only bothered to make use of this facility a few times, as we considered it much better to do our laundering in the yard. Every Saturday night we would pump buckets of water to fill the old copper, and accumulate the logs required for the fire underneath to heat the water. Before breakfast on Sunday one of us would dive out to the washhouse and get the fire going, so that as soon as breakfast was out of the way we could make a start.

There was enough hot water in the copper for us each to have a bucket of suds, and we would kneel on the cobbles, splashing about until a fair portion of the threshing dust was floating on the water. It was possible to lay the washed bits on the stones while we emptied the mud down the drain, and pumped clean water for rinsing, because all the splashing and overflowing during the washing session cleaned off any dust from the cobbles. When it was all rinsed, we pegged it with strong gipsy pegs to the line, hauled it high in the air, and watched with pride as the wind caught it and blew it freely in the clean country air. There was often space to spare on the long line, and we would do towels or tea cloths from Mrs Bird's 'soiled' box, so that on occasions the finished load was so heavy that it took our quite considerable combined muscle to heave it up by the props.

Wet or fine, we did our laundry this way and, in the beginning, Mrs Bird would worry about it. I am sure she thought us quite mad, but we had to bike to and from the farms and work out in all weathers, and we never caught colds after the first few months. Poor Mrs Bird, she could not understand the pleasure we got from having so much space to do the job, from seeing the white bits actually staying white, and from sniffing the lovely fresh smell of the articles when they had dried in the air. I am sure the good lady would have had a fit if she could have seen the way our mothers had to cope with their mountains of washing in the confines of the kitchen-cum-everything else, and she certainly had no idea what it was like to hang things out clean and wet and get them in later dry and smelly. As for my mum, she thought it totally 'PRIMITIVE' to have to pump water. To do all the business outside and in public was quite beyond her ken.

These two wonderful ladies, with such completely different ways of life, had absolutely no conception of each other and it was fairly certain they would never meet. It was a strange feeling to be 'in the gap', shifting from one world to another.

Chapter 19

After our first few weekends with her, Mrs Bird suddenly decided on the Sunday morning that she would resume her normal practice of going to Church for the morning service. Out came the best hat and coat, and the Prayer Book, and in no time at all she was ready. On her way out, almost as an afterthought, she asked, or rather, stated: "You girls will be able to start the lunch, won't you?" "Of course," we assured her, and it was only after she had gone that it dawned on us that we had very little idea of what there was planned for the meal nor where the ingredients were kept!

We had all taken the standard cookery course at school in our time, and had learned how to make bread (after a fashion), create cream horns (total disasters) and perform other equally unsuccessful projects, but the lessons were not long enough, (or perhaps the teachers were not brave enough) to tackle a useful item like a common or garden meal.

As for the opportunity to learn at home, that was no go from the beginning. With so little space, mothers tended to clear the room when they had cooking to do. It just was not feasible, or safe, to have children underfoot while the range was hot and boiling pots were being transferred to and from it in such limited walking space. Apart from this, we were not familiar with where things were kept in Mrs Bird's kitchen. We had to embark on a voyage of discovery, opening doors and drawers, until we came upon the walk-in larder. This veritable treasure house contained more food than we had seen other than at our local grocer's shop. It held enough to keep a battalion of soldiers happy for a good long time!

We found a large chicken, trussed and ready for the pot, some potatoes and carrots in sacks on the tiled floor, and on a shelf, near to the bird, a huge round pie, made but uncooked. Setting to with a will, we stoked the fire, put the chicken in the oven, and, as an afterthought, put in the pie as well, thinking it was probably the dessert. We peeled potatoes and carrots, but when we had filled a pot of each, we felt the meal lacked variety. Ellie remembered that

she had seen cabbages growing in the garden, so we all trooped out to investigate. The largest of the cabbages was right in the centre of the patch, and Dolly, armed with a spade she had found in the shed, climbed over the other cabbages and proceeded to unearth the giant in the middle. It left rather a big crater, and the surrounding plants developed a decided list towards the hole, but, we thought, they were probably only temporarily 'shocked'.

When the cabbage was washed and chopped up, we placed all the pans on the hob, and surveyed our handiwork with considerable satisfaction. It was as we were laying the table that Ellie had a thought about the pudding, to wit, how much nicer that pie would be with some custard. She thought she knew how to make it, and a search in the larder resulted in the discovery of a tin of custard powder and a deep canful of milk, just the job. We were extremely proud of our achievements, and sat back on our laurels waiting for the squeals of delight when Mrs Bird returned home and saw how well we had done.

A good housewife needs to be very well in control of herself to be able to walk into a disaster area without blowing her top. She kept cool as she removed a charred bird (cooked without fat) from the oven, together with a black-topped (meat) pie that had been prepared for tomorrow's dinner. She dashed around, still in her going-to-church outfit, replacing water in the boiled-dry saucepans of vegetables. She, kind soul that she was, did not bat a single eyelid at the sight of the jugful of custard-coloured lumps! Our Mrs Bird did all of these things and she even made no comment when half the cabbages around the crater began to wilt. She skipped the next couple of Sunday Church sessions to 'take us in hand', and we had some much needed tuition in how to produce an appetising meal successfully. Once we knew what we were doing, we thoroughly enjoyed our sessions in the kitchen during her absence.

It was thanks to her ingenuity and expertise in the kitchen, and the kindness of her sons, that we were fed so well in that house. One of her sons had a small farm, mainly running poultry, but keeping a couple of bacon pigs and a cow for home use. Whenever a pig was sent to the bacon factory we were presented with a joint, while surpluses of milk, and the cracked eggs that could not be sent away, found their way into our larder too. The surplus milk was carefully skimmed, and butter churned from it to make certain that we had plenty for our sandwiches, with enough left over for the delicate pies and cakes that Mrs Bird was so good at making.

One of the other sons was in charge of pest control, as he had been a gamekeeper on a big estate before the war. He worked for the Ministry of Agriculture, and his job was of major importance to the war effort. While the U-Boats were blockading Britain, we had to rely almost entirely on home-grown production to feed everyone. In consequence every green thing growing in fields, most of all the grain, were very precious commodities. Unfortunately, with so many of the gamekeepers and farm workers in the armed forces, wildlife in general had got out of hand. Pigeons, rabbits, squirrels, mice, rats and many other species went forth and multiplied (as instructed in the good book) without let or hindrance, and, every new generation needed feeding. They fed on human requirements, the grain, the vegetables and the fruit, so the pest controllers played a vital role in keeping the numbers down, and protecting our food supply.

This, thanks to Albert Bird, was an indirect benefit to us. When he had had a successful day, there would be a rabbit or two in the larder, or perhaps a brace of wild pheasant, or even a hare — good eating in the capable hands of our landlady. In this way we were introduced to many new tastes to sample, and we agreed we had never eaten so varied and nourishing a diet before.

There was only one occasion that I was unable to face the food placed in front of me, and that was entirely my own silly squeamishness. In our backyard at home there had always been a two-tiered, mesh-fronted shed, the lower half housing a few scruffy chickens, fed entirely on scraps and peelings, who once in a while laid eggs, while the top layer of the shed housed my father's pride and joy, a flight of pigeons. Dad had an amazing rapport with his birds and he spent hours sitting on the roof of the shed watching them fly. He had a long pole, which he would slowly twirl in a circle above his head, and those pigeons, flying free as the air, would circle in whichever direction the pole was going. People seeing this for the first time often said that the birds would probably be doing this anyway, and that it had no connection with my Dad's actions, but then he would just change the direction of the pole, and the birds would turn around too. When he felt that they had had enough exercise, he only needed to lay down the pole, and one by one they would flutter down to the roof beside him, to be petted and fed before returning to their roost, quite voluntarily.

From early childhood I have memories of those lovely birds eating from my none-too-gentle hands. Because of this, although reason told me that the two purple-coloured lumps on my plate at Mrs Bird's were totally different from my father's tame pigeons, that they devastated the crops and needed to be culled for their own good as well as the country's, my hands refused to lift the knife and fork to the pathetic little corpses. That was the only time I turned my face away from an un-emptied plate in more than two years with Mrs Bird, and it says it all about the way she looked after us.

Chapter 20

In the beginning it had seemed to be a major catastrophe when, as often happened, we caught our dungarees on a sharp thatching peg, or ripped open a seam somewhere during all the twisting and turning that was an integral part of our job. We also went through at the knees, or poked a toe through a sock, with sickening regularity. Sewing was another item on the ever-lengthening list of things we were discovering for ourselves to be useless at, and our egos were taking a real bashing as all these inefficiencies came, one after another, to our reluctant notice. I remember how shamefaced I was to have to admit that, apart from quite disastrous attempts at making a baby's dress in the sewing lessons at school (when I spent three-quarters of the session unpicking the mistakes I had made in the first quarter), I had never sewn anything in my whole life!

As I was the youngest of four girls, the hand-me-downs, by the time they reached my level, were on their last mission, and not strong enough to bear the ministrations of needle and thread when they were torn. When I started work, and was clothing myself from my meagre wage packet, I had of necessity to buy cheap and flimsy, always hoping that the article would hang together until I had saved enough to buy something else. My mother was a poor needle-woman, and her feeble cobble-ups offered little incentive to us to try to make things last longer.

In the Land Army, things were completely different. To get replacements of anything meant 'going through channels' to ensure that all requests were authentic. Even when an item had literally fallen apart, or worn threadbare, and new items were granted, the wait for their arrival was usually weeks. So patching and darning were the order of the day, and our early attempts added considerably to our 'raggle-taggle-gipsy' look. I remember Ellie proudly producing two reels of cotton (one black and one white) and a pack of darning needles, after a weekend visit home. The colours of the cotton were rather a drawback, as all our most vulnerable items were fawn or brown, making invisibility an impossible aim. We were not too worried by ruched or frilly patches in dungarees or overall coats inserted with white or black stitching — threshing soon obliterated them anyway. But it was quite painful to be stuck with socks that had gathered bunches in the heel and toe areas and, after a day of agony, the worst one of a pair would be set aside and replaced by a whole or nearly whole one. Eventually, when we had reached the point where there WERE no more good ones, we admitted defeat, and begged Mrs Bird to give us a few hints.

Finding some wool and cotton to match our uniform issue, she set about giving us a course of no-nonsense mending and, after weeks of concentrated effort, our socks began to emerge with proper darns that retained the original shapes of heels and toes, were quite flat, and above all were comfortable to wear. Having mastered darning, we went on to strong neat patches (with fawn cotton stitching) and were surprised to find how much less of a chore it seemed when the end result was bearable to look at, as well as undetectable in the wearing.

Mrs Bird was remarkably patient with us throughout all the trial and error period. It was always one of us who got angry and threw our failures on the floor in frustration! When I commented on this one day after a particularly stormy outburst from Ellie had provoked only a very mild "Tut tut" from her, she just gave one of her cheeky grins as she replied, "You think YOU'RE hard to teach? You should have seen the fuss and bother I had with my boys!"

Yes indeed, she had actually taught her 'hulking great sons' all the domestic arts, exactly as if they had been girls. In town, a man washing, ironing, cooking or sewing would have been quite automatically classified as a cissy, but having seen two of Mrs Bird's extremely manly 'boys', we were obliged yet again to adjust our prejudices.

We spent a great deal of our spare time writing letters, as did most people who were parted from relatives and friends, and we knew how important letters were to those away on active service. Di had an incredible number of penpals. I think every soldier she had ever been out with corresponded with her after being moved on. Ellie, of course, was forever writing to her Frank, and Dolly had a string of relations serving abroad.

I acquired a very good friend by pure chance. I had written several letters to my older brother (then serving in France) without receiving any replies when, one day, I arrived home from work to find a Forces letter in a handwriting I did not recognise. It was from the office doing censor service in the area in France where my brother's unit had been. It was part of his job to inspect all letters to ensure they held no information that could be of use to the enemy if they should fall into the wrong hands. After reading my cheery offerings to my brother, he had felt a sudden urge to write to me himself.

That was the beginning of a friendship that I came to treasure. He was a really nice man, ten years my senior and, from the way he wrote, it was plain to see how very different his up-bringing had been to my own, but the difference in our ages and backgrounds did not seem to be important at all. We found we had a similar wacky sense of humour and, when I wrote of some of our experiences on the farms, he found them very funny. I think writing to Harold made me feel more mature, and less of a scatter-brain, while my letters cheered him through the 'grim bits' (as he termed the unmentionable aspects of his situation).

We always hoped to meet when the war was over. "I'll show you the London town you've missed out on," he promised. "We'll paint it redder than it's ever been painted before!" Sadly, we did not get the chance, because, after he had been writing for over a year, his letters suddenly stopped coming, and although I had no official notification (not being related), I knew my poor old Harold was one of the many who would not see the peace, or paint anything red, blue, or any other colour at all. I realised then, for the first time really, if I was feeling so bereft about someone I had never met, how much worse it must be for wives and mothers who lost their dear ones.

It was about that time that Di lost two of her ex-boyfriend/penfriends, and Ellie lost contact, for a while, with her Frank. We all needed something to take our minds off the war for a bit — but what to do? At home the free public library was in constant use by all my family, except Dad, but here in the country a mobile van came only infrequently round the villages. Being such enthusiastic readers, we had exhausted its stock of our own personal choices of reading matter in no time at all.

One evening as we sat twiddling our thumbs, Mrs Bird came into the sitting room, looked at our glum faces, and told us, "When I was a girl about your ages, I never had any moments when I was as bored as you lot are. I could get really engrossed in my sewing, and my mother often needed to ORDER me to stop, when she thought it was tiring my eyes." Our reaction to her suggestion was to reject it out of hand, and we all told stories of disastrous efforts at making things when we were at school.

"Oh NO! — I didn't like doing that sort of work either!" she told us. "I meant pleasure sewing, embroidering! You wouldn't believe how fascinating it can be, watching a picture develop stitch by stitch." This was something else we had missed out on, and we had doubts of our abilities to make something of it, but on our way home from work the next day, we stopped off at the tiny Post Office. This doubled as many other things, one of which was a handicraft centre. One quick look round impressed us. We came away with squares of cheap crash material, crewel needles and a few skeins of brightly coloured silks.

It took us a while to decide on the pictures we wanted to create (during which time we discovered hidden talents in the designing field), but when we had roughly sketched the picture onto the material, Mrs Bird taught us some very basic embroidery stitches.

There were no more 'glum-faced evenings', as we sat and struggled to make our coarse, calloused fingers manipulate the needles and fine silk. Ellie and Dolly made floral designs, and I began a very ambitious project, a galleon in full sail. These pictures in silk kept us occupied all through the long winter evenings, and the sense of satisfaction and pride when we eventually put in the final stitches was really great! Works of art they were NOT, but they were all our own.

Chapter 21

Bill and Bert, like a lot of the older farm people, were real tough guys regarding the weather. They made few concessions to heat and cold, wearing little extra in the winter and taking little, if anything, off in the summer.

Bill told us one day that Bert, in all his fifty years, had never worn socks or underclothing. Come what might, he faced the world in hobnail boots, faded serge trousers, a check workshirt with no collar and an ancient tweed jacket which never came off except on the very hottest days, and was only ever buttoned up for the bike rides to and from his home in the winter. Neither of them wore macs or caps, nor did they need 'sissy bits and bobs' like scarves and gloves. Just once in a while, if it was really bitterly cold, we might see Bill warm his hands on the engine boiler, but that did not happen often. We envied them their seeming lack of weather-consciousness, as we froze or sweated, piled on everything we had, or stripped off as much as possible.

Watching them eat their lunches was an education, and we believed their diet could have a lot to do with their insulation against all weathers. They both invariably brought the same, day in, day out. A hunk of bread, a wedge of cheese, for Bert a raw onion, and for Bill a big green cooking apple. They would first peel the apple/onion with quite evil-looking pocket knives, then out would come the bread and cheese, and somehow they managed to hold the three items in one hand while chopping a piece of each, then pop them all into the mouth from the knife with the other hand. We had a couple of goes at doing this ourselves, but it was obviously an achievement needing years of practice, and as food was too precious to drop all over farmyards, we gave up on it.

They never caught colds or flu, even when the germs were rampant in others on the farms, nor did they ever have time off work for sickness of any kind in all the time we knew them, so this unchanging diet must have been a very healthy one.

Years after the war I chanced upon Bill at a steam engine rally, and it was like turning back the clock. He looked no older, was dressed in much the same manner and, at the time I spotted him, had just sat down to his lunch beside the old steam engine. As you have probably guessed, his lunch was a hunk of bread, a wedge of cheese, and a big sour green cooking apple, cut and 'forked' into his mouth by the same old knife.

Both our fellow workers were just about the most even-tempered men we had ever had to deal with. Bert, the born philosopher, accepted most adversities with stoical calm, but he never went over the top about the good things either. We never met his wife, but felt she must be a very understanding lady to be content with his complete lack of enthusiasm, and his air of docile acceptance, whatever fate served up. Bill, on the other hand, did take notice of things that went wrong and was known to grumble sometimes. He had a great sense of humour, and fanatical enthusiasm for all things connected with steam engines.

In all the time I knew them, Bill was the only one I saw really lose his temper, and that only happened once. We had just finished threshing a huge stack of black beans and the machine, like the area all around it, was filthy with black sooty dust. The concave drum in the interior was gunged up with bits of black stalk and pods, dust and mouldy leaves, and Bert had decreed it should be cleaned out before we moved on to the next farm, where we had a clean crop to thresh. So while Bill went off to find a clean water supply for refilling the engine boiler, Bert laid himself out over the drum cavity, reaching down with a handbrush to clean off the inside, which usually whizzed round at such a speed as to be virtually invisible, and we cleaned off sieves and brushed out dust from all accessible belts, ledges and cavities.

Bill's shouts of anger startled us all! Bert's head popped up out of the drum, and we came out from the places we had currently been cleaning at the rear end of the machine to see what had stirred our usually calm Bill to such extremes. He was racing across the adjacent field waving his fist, and shouting wildly, and when we looked towards the steam engine, we saw the reason for this unusual display. The farmer, an arrogant, inconsiderate man at all times, had broken the strict ruling that no one except those of us qualified to do so messed about with the machine or the engine.

As Bill had been coming back from his search for water, he saw the farmer's two sons, aged six and eight years, standing in the engine box. One, the younger, was playing with the steering wheel, while the bigger one was hauling on a lever. By chance it happened to be the lever that started the drive wheel that turned the belt to work the thresher. Had he succeeded in moving it into gear (which, due to Bill's conscientious regularity with the oil can, was possible) most of us, who had fingers, hands or whole arms in places inaccessible when the machine was in motion, would surely have suffered serious injury. Bert, with his upper half suspended in the drum, would have lost both arms, and possibly his life. The drive belt, for safety's sake, was usually the first thing to be taken off when we started packing up, but had been left in operational position on this day so that Bill could give just a short spin to dispel the bits and dust after we had loosened them.

The farmer, standing beside the engine after lifting the boys onto it, was deeply affronted when Bill unceremoniously whipped them off, but Bill was so angry that he battered down the man's spluttered excuses with his tirade. When the dust had settled, so to speak, and we were all packed up and raring to go, the farmer's wife brought us tea, and we sat briefly on some straw bales to drink it, as we all, especially Bert, expressed our gratitude for Bill's prompt recognition, and averting, of the dangerous situation. The still rather pale and shaken Bill gave one of his wry grins, "I was only thinking of the lad," he told us, "we couldn't let him go through his whole life with you lot on his conscience, could we?"

Wherever possible, farmers would stack some of their harvest in barns, for with walls on at least one side and a roof for shelter, they could pile it much higher, sometimes right up to the roof. This was never popular with anyone when it came to the threshing of the grain, as the machine had to be inside the barn too, and in the enclosed space the din was unimaginable, the dust hung in the air, and everyone got very hot.

It was also more beset with danger, as the girl on the top of the pile needed to throw the sheaves an extra distance to the machine. Accuracy of aim was more difficult, and whoever was on the machine cutting bonds risked being knocked over by a misjudged, heavy sheaf or, if her arm was jogged, suffering a nasty gash from the razor sharp hooked knife.

One elderly farmer was always most concerned for our safety on the heights, "You be careful up there my gal," he would call, as we climbed the ladders, "if you come down from up top you'll kill yourself for sure!" Of course we did not need telling; we were all well aware of the dangers, and I always thought, being the coward I was, I would be the last one to take any chances. I found I was wrong about that one day.

It was my turn on top in a barn which had been stacked so high we dare not risk the long drop to the machine, and the farmer had installed an intermediary hand on a wagon piled high with bales of straw, so the sheaves went down in two more manageable stages. We had just taken up our various positions, and were waiting for the machine to start up, when we heard the all too familiar sound of a doodlebug on its way to batter poor old London a bit more. Only this one must have been wrongly primed, because when it was right overhead the engine cut out, and that we all knew meant only one thing, it was on its way down!

And so was I! Without thought or hesitation I threw myself off the top of the pile onto the loaded wagon, rolled to the edge, and jumped the fifteen to twenty feet to the ground. After the wretched bomb had exploded close by, the rest of the workforce were surprised to see me alongside as they picked themselves up off the floor, and they found it hard to believe I had managed to get down voluntarily. If I had not jumped, the shock waves of the explosion would almost certainly have blown me off, so my impetuous, highly dangerous acrobatics had in all probability saved my life.

Chapter 22

I had been on the threshing machine for almost three years and would have been quite content to stay with Bill, Bert and the gang and billet with our dear Mrs Bird till the end of the war but, out of the blue, there was trouble at home.

My father, never very strong, was suddenly taken ill and rushed into hospital for an emergency operation. All the local hospitals had been cleared for air-raid casualties and civilians with ordinary illnesses were sent out of London to whatever nursing homes, cottage hospitals or similar establishments could be utilised as general hospitals.

My mother was herself due to go into hospital for an operation but, in view of the serious condition of my dad, she postponed her own admission. She was not well enough to make the journey to visit my father alone under wartime conditions, and this presented a difficulty.

All the family were away from home, some overseas, and my eldest sister had been conscripted to work in a munitions factory at a secret location somewhere in the north of England. So I was the obvious one to help my mother, but my problem was getting back after visiting, which was confined to just two hours on Sunday afternoons. As previously mentioned, because of the early hour at which the country buses stopped running, I had to start my return journey immediately after lunch.

It seemed that the only way around this was to apply for transfer to somewhere more accessible to London. The Land Army were very good on this point, sending me to a hostel at South Darenth near Dartford, five minutes walk from the mainline station, and with a service that continued late into the evening.

I was really very sad to have to leave all my friends, but it was a relief to know that I was going to be in such a good position to help my mother, and I was settled into the hostel within a week of applying. I found it a very different option to living in a billet, and I am sure that in less worrying circumstances I would have enjoyed the change. It was situated in a beautiful old house standing in extensive grounds, and was reminiscent of stories I had read about private schools.

The bedrooms, which occupied two floors, were huge and comfortably accommodated five or six beds, which contributed to the illusion of school. There were three bathrooms for each floor to share, their facilities being extended by extra baths and basins in each. They were so spacious that there was plenty of room for the additions.

The girls were mostly new recruits, younger than I, and they were enjoying themselves in this free-from-home-restraint atmosphere. Noisy and boisterous, they were forever playing practical jokes among themselves, their favourite being the vanishing towel trick when they were washing or bathing in the communal bathrooms. There would result screams of laughter, and pounding on doors, as the deprived one ran from room to room, dripping and nude, looking for the culprit.

In more normal circumstances I might have been tempted to join in the fun but, with so much on my mind, it was a relief to be allocated a small twin-bedded room in the servants' wing. The whole of this area was separated from the main house by two heavy doors, covered in baize, that quite effectively cut us off from the high jinks in the main part. The girl I shared with always had her head stuck in a book which, in my present mood, suited me just fine.

Our days were well regimented by the clock and the gong. We were up at 5.30, breakfast at 6.00 sharp, and the lorry picked us up *en masse* at 6.30. At 5.30 every afternoon our driver came back to pick us up from whatever location he had dropped us at in the morning, and we had time to clean up before dinner at 7.00 p.m. The meals were good, nourishing and varied, and there were never any plates that had not been completely emptied afterwards. When dinner was over, we filed through a kind of servery, where long tables were loaded with trays of sandwiches, each tray bearing instructions on how many of its variety each of us should take. After we had completed our journey round the tables, and packed our 'one-per-person/two-per-person' rations for the next day into our sizable lunchboxes, we stowed them on our chairs in the dining room, ready to pick up after breakfast next day.

There had been times when the old gang bemoaned the lack of variety in our lunches. Cheese was the only extra ration our landladies received, enormous great wedges of it, and of course the logical way to make use of it was to bung it in our sandwiches, but it did get a bit boring at times.

The reverse was the case at the hostel, where we had so much variety, under the one-per-person routine, that there would be an exchange session in the lorry most mornings, "Anyone want a cheese for a Spam?" — or a Marmite, or a Peanut butter — until we had all, more or less, obtained a variety containing the kinds of filling we liked best. This barter needed to be done before we arrived, because no one wanted handled food once we had started work.

During most of the time I was at the hostel we were lifting potatoes or sugar-beet. Large areas of common ground were ploughed for the war effort, and it was considered advisable that the first crop on this long-uncultivated soil should be a hardy root like potatoes, as the process of digging up the crop also removed many of the weed roots established in the soil. Thus it was cleaned for the next, more useful, cropping of wheat, oats or barley.

Our worst place was on the recently drained Swanscombe Marsh near the Thames Estuary. The crop had been lifted and built into clamps sometime previously, then an extra high tide flooded over the top of the embankment, and the potato storage clamps were inundated with sea water. This had made the crop unfit for human consumption, but we had to sort through for those tubers suitable for animal feed. It was far from pleasant, with slimy mud still underfoot in spite of renewed drainage operations in progress, and the potatoes were mostly a squadgy, mucky mess!

It was a strange sensation to be working on the marsh looking up to the top of the high embankment on the riverside, seeing the masts and funnels of ships going by, and it was one of these ships that caused a great deal of discomfort to us. We were all working round one of the long, heaped-up storage clamps of rotting spuds when there was a loud, whining sort of whistle noise, and a terrific CRACK! "Get down everyone," the forewoman yelled, "Some blighter's shooting at us!" She could have saved her breath! We had all had some experience of the Blitz and knew, all too well, the drill when danger threatened. We had all instinctively thrown ourselves to the ground. Perhaps the chap who fired that shot

found it funny. We certainly did not — especially when we had picked ourselves up off the deck, seen the slimy mud all over us, and got a whiff of the rotten potatoes we had squelched ourselves down in. We had to stay plastered until the lorry came for us, and there was a mad stampede for the bathrooms upon our arrival at the hostel. We just could not wait to rid ourselves of that dreadful pong!

It was during our spell on this marshy place that our worst practical joker got her come-uppance. The hostel jokes were usually played, and taken, lightheartedly, but there was one girl (isn't there always?) who could not resist taking things just that bit too far, so that they ceased to be funny.

When the gong sounded to wake us in the mornings, it allowed just about the right amount of time for us to wash, clean our teeth, dress and be down in the dining hall as the breakfasts started coming through the hatch. On this particular morning, loud squeals and shrieks of rage coming from Betty's room made everyone rush to their doorway to find out what was wrong. During the night when her room-mates were asleep, Betty had crept around the room mixing up their clothing, so that tall girls had short dungarees, the fat one could not get into anything, and the shorter ones absolutely floated in outsize tent look-alikes. As everything was uniform, it took quite a time to sort out and, in consequence, these five girls had to miss most of their breakfast.

Everyone, knowing the culprit must have been Betty (the silly girl had omitted to cover her tracks by mixing up some of her own things), waited for reprisals, but nothing was said, although we could see that the five were simmering. We decided that their ploy was to ignore what had happened, which is often quite the most frustrating reaction to a joker like Betty.

The next morning, however, the word went round "No sandwich exchanges on the lorry please." We were all asked to stick with what we had got, just for this one day. We waited impatiently, dying to see what would happen when we sat down for our lunch at mid-day. It was the custom for us all to form a circle sitting on some old crates we had found, and so it was very difficult, from any position, not to let one's eyes stray in Betty's direction.

Our landlady was no doubt influenced by the strange household. Almost as odd as they were, she fitted in well: the house and its occupants would have done Alfred Hitchcock a favour!

Now Betty was a trifle uncouth in habits, especially as regards eating. Our sandwiches were formed by cutting one slice straight across and folding over cornerwise, but Betty would fold hers again, making it a very thick quarter slice. By taking one massive bite, she would be left with just the crusts for the follow up. She did this with the first sandwich on this day of retribution, and then, as the taste reached her palate, she snorted like an angry horse, choked, and then spat out the lot! She tasted the next one very gingerly, but that one was O.K. and, obviously thinking that only the first one had been 'doctored', she began eating heartily again. Nemesis had been quite crafty, however, and the few that had been 'got at' were well mixed in with the rest, so Betty, for a change, ate her food very daintily, nibbling each sandwich with the utmost caution!

Nothing was ever mentioned about the return 'joke', and we never did find out what had been added to make the food taste so vile, but we were all amazed at the effect it had on Betty. She retired from the arena, spending her evenings lying on her bed with a book, or writing letters, and there were no more sting-in-the-tail jokes from her all the rest of the time I was there.

On Sundays I went with my mother to visit Dad in hospital, and there was ample time for us to get home and have tea together before I needed to catch my train. It was a comfort to us both that I could get home so quickly, especially when my father died.

I was given a week's compassionate leave, to help Mum through the funeral and to see her into hospital on the day after it, for her own operation, but it was obvious a week was not going to be sufficient. My mother would need someone at home to help her for a goodly time after her major surgery. The Ministry people decided that the best option was to release my elder sister from her munitions commitment, allowing her to live at home, while doing other essential war-work in the locality. As soon as Mary was released, I received my marching orders, and within a few days it was back to threshing again.

Chapter 23

The old gang was complete, and Mrs Bird's complement of girls was full, but, even had there been a vacancy, I would not have been the one to fill it. I was needed to start a new gang in another part of Kent, with three girls who had no experience of threshing, and a one-man, tractor-driven machine.

We were all billeted together in a house in Hawkhurst that had once been a laundry. It was a three-storey building, unusual in a village, and it did not feel at all home-like, but rather empty. The top floor was divided into two mini-flats, occupied by other more long term lodgers. A rather odd woman with a small child, evacuated from London we deduced, who crept about rarely speaking to anyone, lived in the bigger of these flats. The other housed a spinster lady who was just the reverse of silent! She had a strange urge to speak with passers-by in the street, practically living by her window so that none would be missed. To make herself heard from that height, she needed to shout and, when the person on the street spoke too softly in reply, it was a common, if terrifying, sight to see this dear lady hanging out of her window the better to hear, and very likely to fall in our opinion. The second floor in this strange house consisted of our large bedroom, a bathroom (with cold running water) and, at the end of a long passageway, surrounded by empty rooms, our landlady's bedroom.

There were more empty rooms on the ground floor, which had been the main work area of the laundry, and the gas cooker stood in splendid isolation in one of these chill, bare rooms, across the hall from the only one furnished, which was Mrs Street's sitting/dining room.

She meant well, and we did feel welcome, which compensated for the oddities. The lady had no sense of smell at all, a defect from birth she told us, and this proved quite a drawback, especially when cooking. Our mealtimes were always approached with caution, and a degree of uncertainty — would our food be half raw — or was it a done-to-death day?

The only concession we received from the Food Ministry for the toughness of the work was the extra cheese ration, and with four of us, Mrs Street's allocation was a huge lump! But Mrs Street had a friend who had access to vast quantities of dried egg (via the very efficient black market we suspected) and the good ladies did a regular swap, some of our cheese mountain for a supply of dried egg. Consequently our breakfast was invariably leather-textured over-cooked (or under-done at times) scrambled eggs. The remaining cheese went into our sandwiches, but at least, to give her her due, the old dear did attempt to add variety to these by dousing them with different sauces.

One day when we went to eat our lunch, we found it so revolting that we just could not eat a single bite. Mrs Street had intended to treat us to a tasty garnish, Worcester sauce, a bit of a rarity in the shops, but obtained through her friend the black market lady. Unfortunately, in her usual state of 'other-worldliness', she had picked up the wrong bottle, and our cheese was heavily drenched in Camp coffee — definitely not a mixture to be advocated!

In her own strange way Mrs Street tried to do her best for us, although she did try to work a fiddle when we first arrived. It happened because the cooker, with its meter, was in a room across the hall from the living room downstairs, and Mrs Street had told us we could have as much hot water as we liked, but would be expected to replenish the meter when it ran out. The meter would only accept one shilling coins (five pence) but we reasoned that it should be within our means if we only used one small kettleful each for our evening ablutions. It just seemed an unfortunate coincidence that the meter needed to be fed when we went down for our first lot, but assuming that our meal had run it down, we put in our shilling.

I boiled my kettleful, carried it up to the bathroom on the second floor and, after I had emptied it for my wash, passed it on to Valerie. But when she went down to boil it for herself, the gas was all used up again! Just one small kettleful for a whole shilling's worth? We could not believe it!

It was very obvious that we could not afford a shilling each every night, so we had to opt for cold water washes and laundry, unless one of us had spare money to fritter on that greedy meter.

About three days later, we came home from work exceptionally dirty, having had a day of threshing black cattle beans, and it had been bitterly cold to boot. Unable to face ice-cold water for the overall wash we needed we counted our combined resources and found we could just afford one kettle of hot water amongst us. It should, at least, take the chill off.

Sally popped down with the kettle and the meter shilling, but as it was really cold in that empty room, she did not wait for it to boil. It usually took about five minutes so, after allowing this, I volunteered to go down to collect it. I had no intention of hanging around on that concrete floor, so I did not bother to put my discarded shoes back on. Thus my approach down the stairs in stockinged feet was undetected by the very crafty old lady dashing across the hall from the cooker room to her living room, laden with a large saucepan and kettle, hissing steam! Our kettle, barely warm when I reached it, had not quite achieved boiling point when the gas fizzled out. After that eye-opener, we washed in cold water all the time, and in fact became so used to it that on one of my weekends at home I startled my mother when, without thinking, I started to run the cold water for my wash.

The girls in my new gang were all new to threshing, though they had been on other tasks in the Land Army for several years. Although we made a go of it, we none of us felt the same urge to shine as had my first gang. We, the first gang, had successfully proved that women could do the job, and now the challenge was missing; most threshing machines had their own, accepted, gang of girls. There was not even the need to get used to living away from home, discovering the good and bad points of country living and learning to ride the bikes. We had got through all that, and were somewhat blasé about the whole thing. I think belonging to the old gang had spoilt me and although the new girls were a pleasant bunch to have as workmates, I could not find the old spirit of camaraderie with them.

I missed the messy old steam engine too. We had an old Fordson tractor to drive this thresher, and our man in charge, Mr Johnson, was not at all like Bill and Bert. He was a bit of a mystery in fact, and we found it hard to understand how he had got the job. It was obvious he was not a countryman, with those soft, pudgy hands and pale face. He would have looked more in his element with a rolled umbrella and briefcase. He could drive the tractor, which for a car driver would not be difficult, but his knowledge of the working of the machines was very limited indeed. Once he realised that I was fairly experienced, a lot of the technical work such as the changing of sieves for different kinds of grain threshing, trusser repairs and other minor jobs of that ilk fell to me. I really do not know how he would have got by if the gang had been all rookies.

As it happened, when things needed doing he was vary rarely about anyway — we would get the machines set up ready to go on a new farm, and then as soon as work began our Mr Johnson would borrow one of our bikes to "Go and get my car from the last place", or would say "I've got to go to a meeting". Sometimes it was only a phone call he had to make, but in all instances an errand that would take a normal person an hour at most usually lasted our boss for most of the day. He was not popular with the farmers of course; they could have done without his skiving off, and even more so when something went wrong that my very basic knowledge could not cope with, which was mainly tractor trouble. I knew absolutely nothing about tractor engines, and with the 'man in charge' noticeable mostly by his absence, the farmers often had to take one of their own mechanics off some other job to come and fix our tractor.

We had no Bert with this outfit, as the tractor did not need the constant attention that the steam engine had. Once started it could run on its own, which in theory should have left the driver free to take on the feeding into the machine, something Bert had always done. But our driver, apart from his frequent absences, was not terribly keen to chance his arm on this and, as most farm workers took the same attitude, it fell more and more into my lap.

Valerie was the 'beauty queen' of our group, very eye-catching, with her fair skin and blonde hair. If she could cajole a workman to swap places with her when it was her turn for the dirty business of the cavel raking, she would be in high spirits, but when it did not work she would be in a sulky mood all day. Valerie's looks were of prime importance to Valerie, and although she had agreed that the turn system was a good one, giving everyone a break and spreading the unpleasant tasks, she never gave up trying to get out of taking her turn.

Our vain beauty really hit bottom in bad behaviour one day. It was Saturday, at the end of a long hard week of struggling with the weather. Everything was frozen solid, and there was quite heavy snow. All through the morning Valerie had been complaining of stomach ache, but she had carried on working until, just after our mid-day break, she suddenly doubled over, "Can someone take over," she groaned, "I really hurt!"

We helped her to the nearby barn, and let her sit out of the weather for a while until she said she felt well enough to cope with the bike ride back to the billet. We were so short-handed, even more so now that she was off, that there was no way I could spare another of the girls to ride with her, and I spent the next hour or so worrying whether she had made it back safely.

We were just stopping for our three o'clock tea break when Jo, who was at the top of the cornstack, shouted, "Hey! Would you just look at that!" Following her pointing finger, I looked towards the lane that ran beside the field we were in — just in time to see a cleaned-up, beaming Valerie, floating by on the top deck of a bus that had slowed down round a bend!

Of course, the farmer had also seen her, and he was most angry with me, quite sure that this was a put up job to get one of us off early. The final straw for me, when we got back to the billet rather later than we would have been if we had not been so short-handed, was a note I found on my bed. It read "Thanks a lot! — see you tomorrow night!" The whole pantomime had been a con trick to give Valerie a longer weekend!

Chapter 24

Life at the old laundry was not all peace and quiet by a long chalk, and the other lodgers contributed to many of the upheavals. The evacuee lady on the top floor must, before her exodus from the capital, have led rather a chequered life, if the number of gentlemen friends who visited at intervals was anything to go by. For one so self-effacing and meek, she had a surprising taste in consorts, all of whom were huge, and frequently ran to violence, both in their speech and in their actions!

Mrs Street grew extremely apprehensive when sounds of discord on the top floor were heard all over the house but, when the slamming front door indicated the departure of yet another irate 'friend', and Lily was next seen with bruises, or a shiner, the poor old dear did not have the heart to give her notice. We suspected that the child caused some of the aggravations. She did not speak much, but when she did open her mouth, she often seemed to say the wrong things and, as her mother confided in one of her rare expansive moods, "Little Gloria can never remember which of her uncles is which" I could see this would be classed as a really major fault in Lily's circumstances!

The other lodger, Miss Mercy, (plain Martha in Mrs Street's book) complained a lot about Lily's noisy visitors. Miss M., however, was not above creating a few diversions herself. A gaunt woman in her mid to late forties, she boasted a boyfriend living locally, and was forever quoting what "My Harry" said, or did. Yet he never called at the house to see her, or to take her out. By the way the poor little man scuttled off down the road when the window was flung open and sweet nothings yelled for all the village to hear as he passed, I think the romance was a distinctly one-sided affair. Even Mrs Street, herself a bundle of nerves, was not completely immune from the maniacal love of making a commotion.

When we were working on old cornstacks towards the end of the season, there would be a fair old collection of live-stock in residence, and we had become quite used to the various bugs and

beetles creeping about as we opened up the stack, letting the harsh light of day reach their hideouts. There would be nests of baby mice and rats galore and, as we neared the base, there would be a mass exodus of everything that could run. The Ministry orders were that all that could be dispatched, should be; the rodents made such inroads on our food supplies. Farmers would encircle the stack with wire netting as we were nearing the end to halt the escapes, and men and dogs would patrol in the enclosed area to ensure their demise.

One evening we popped into the living room as usual to announce our return, and then made to go upstairs to clean up for dinner. But as we turned to the door, Mrs Street started screaming, a piercing, hysterical shriek that went on and on. I turned back towards her to see if I could calm her down (we thought she must be having some kind of a fit) but my action only made the screaming worse.

"It's you she's frightened of!" Valerie shouted, trying to make herself heard above the terrible row, "Stay where you are, and I'll have a go." She put her arms round the old lady, and spoke soothingly. Above the racket it was quite difficult, but eventually

the screams turned to shuddering sobs as, in a cracked voice, Mrs Street pointed an accusing finger at me demanding that I "Go into the garden and strip everything off, at once, this very MINUTE!" Had she gone right off her trolley we wondered? To humour her, I turned to do her bidding, and that was when Jo started to laugh! We thought she had caught the 'crazies' too, until she reached behind me and plucked from the back of my jumper a small, very frightened baby rat! I had ridden more than four miles with this undiscovered pillion passenger, and could only imagine what the poor creature was feeling about that. From then on, a new routine was initiated by the good lady Mrs Street. We were not allowed to enter her part of the house until we had stripped off out in the back garden.

Although Mrs Street was a very hit-and-miss cook, when it came to laundry she was an expert! When her husband had been alive, their business had flourished. They had contracts with a private nursing home, the cottage hospital and several of the big houses in the area. The business had folded upon Mr Street's death, but the old lady still 'obliged' for friends on occasions, and could be found happily ironing and pressing away in the evenings. Piles of sheets, daunting to our eyes, were waded through with vigour. The heaps diminished at great speed, then she would turn to a whole rackful of shirts on hangers. Shirts, in those days, were made on very different lines from modern ones, especially the 'Best' ones. They were pleated from a yoke at the back to allow the wearer flexing space, collars had bone stiffeners and stud holes, and the shaped tails, longer at the rear to give a good tuck-in, certainly aimed to keep the wearer snug, and the ironer busy. Mrs Street made short work of them, neatly 'boxing' the pleats into place, whipping out stiffeners and sliding them back in once the collar was pressed. It was a delight to watch her, especially as she folded the finished article, her old hands moved so quickly. Flat on its back, buttons done up, a flip over onto its front, each side folded into the middle, sleeves turned in and folded over, and then, the final stroke, tail end up first, top folded down over it, and the shirt lay on the table as neatly pressed and immaculately creaseless as on the day it came out of its box brand new!

Mrs Street was quite flattered by my fascination with her expertise, and tried many times to teach me the art, but farm work makes for hefty hands and roughened fingers, and although I tried very hard to achieve at least some measure of efficiency, I made a very poor showing by comparison with Mrs Street.

In one particular respect we found life at Mrs Street's completely different from previous billets. Mrs Bird had been a real country cousin when it came to early rising. We always had a call in ample time to get ourselves ready, with the aroma of our breakfast cooking floating up from the kitchen. In the regimented atmosphere of the hostel where absolutely everything was done by the clock, we also had little to worry about. But Mrs Street was an extremely heavy sleeper, and despite the loudest ringing alarm clock she could find, she could sleep right through its clamour. Even on the rare occasions that she did wake, it was all too frequently set at the wrong time!

Our leaving-for-work time depended on how far we had to travel on any particular day. We could manage with a 6 a.m. rousing when working nearby, but our sphere of operations spread over a five or six mile radius, which meant that there were many times we needed to get up in the region of five o'clock. After a few late arrivals, earning disapproval from farmers kept waiting, we obviously needed to rethink this whole business of waking up in the mornings.

We had no alarm clock ourselves, and Mrs Street was loathe to part with hers, as in her eyes there really WAS no problem. What, after all, did a few odd minutes either way matter? So we decided to try waking ourselves up with the use of the new concept 'auto-suggestion' someone had read about in a book. Before settling down for the night, we all sat staring at our watches, chanting, "We must wake up at five o'clock, we must not oversleep" over and over to get it deeply impressed on our subconscious minds, exactly as the book had directed.

The first night we tried it, none of us slept a wink for worrying about it, but by the second night we were all so tired it did not work at all. However, on the third night, while the others girls went back to the usual 'soon-as-the-head-hits-the-pillow' routine, I woke up every hour on the hour thinking it was time to get up. I really persevered, until one morning I woke with a start to find, to my surprise, that it was exactly the time I had told myself to wake. The girls thought it was coincidence at first but, as time went on and it became automatic, they were rather cross with themselves because they had not been able to master it at all.

I would wake at the prescribed time, wake the other three girls, then paddle up the long empty corridor to Mrs Street's room and, with some difficulty, get her motivated too. It was such a relief not to have to worry about being late again, I did not mind at all when the others gave me the rather derisory nickname 'Old stop-the-clock'. This self-waking system has stood me in good stead throughout the years, and I still manage without an alarm clock.

Chapter 25

For what was to be our last summer hiring (although, of course, we were not to know that at the time) we were sent to a farm that produced, almost exclusively, hops.

Now most beer drinkers go for the end product in a big way, but I doubt very much if many of them realise the absolute, utter awfulness of growing the beastly things — they really are the most vicious brutes! The hop plants (called 'hills') are planted in rows, carefully spaced to leave a gangway wide enough for tractors to traverse, up and down, across and back, almost continuously. The hills last for years so they do not need to be replaced too often.

Poles are spaced at intervals along the rows, supporting a grid of overhead wires with hooks on, and in early spring men with huge balls of coarse string in bags on their backs run the string through the end of these poles, then walk up and down the hop-garden, threading the strings up to an overhead hook, then down to one fixed into the ground near to the plant, until each one has four strings branching out from its base in a cone shape. Women follow the men, carrying great bunches of strings. I said nothing went to waste on farms, these strings were the ones we saved when cutting them off the sheaves on the threshing machine. It just happens they are the right length to tie in the four strings above each hill at about eye level, and this, again, is to make access possible for tractors.

The hop-hills begin growing about March when bunches of bright green trailers called bines shoot out in all directions in the most untidy tangles, twenty or more to each hill. When they have grown to about eighteen inches the 'training' begins. The idea is that eight to ten of the strongest looking shoots are selected, and are separated, untangled, and attempts made to 'twiddle' them up the strings, two or three to each. One thing stands out a mile as soon as you try to do this simple-sounding little lark: hops do not LIKE being organised in this manner. In fact they tend to do battle with the trainer, and fight they certainly can! So rough are their stems that they scratch and tear at weak human flesh, leaving sore, stinging weals and bloodied gashes.

These rebellious shoots having eventually been semi-subdued, the remaining bines have to be weeded out to concentrate all the growth into the select few. Those spare hop bines, however, almost have a mind of their own. They have no intention of leaving the parent plant, hanging on there so that the trainer needs to grip really hard and tug — and off come a few more strips of skin from hands now stained a dirty, unremovable green!

At long last, all the little wretches having been dealt with, the trainer gives a sigh of heartfelt relief. "Thank goodness that's over!" But, of course, it is not! The ones attended to first have been growing like mad, and doing their own thing willy-nilly. The majority have nearly reached the central band of string, and mostly up ONE STRAND! The disappointed trainer gets stuck in again, untangling the thick rope of bines, spacing them out amongst the four strings, and weeding out yet another bush of unwanted growth from the base, carrying on all through the hop-gardens till all are once again tidy — or, ARE they? Back at the beginning again we find that the plants have now passed the central band and, in theory, should be going their separate ways up the diverging strings, above the restraining band. These monsters appear to have an overwhelming desire for 'togetherness' and untangling and relocation is once again required, plus, of course, another bush of unwanted growth to be weeded out from the bottom.

Throughout the whole of the training cycle tractors constantly traverse the alley-ways with special harrows to churn over the soil, keeping it free of weeds, open for drainage, and very uncomfortable to walk on. The bines, after the third realignment, have grown too high to be corrected even if they have gone adrift again, so now comes the 'leaf and weed' operation. All leaves have to be stripped from the central band to the base, leaving just exposed stalks emerging from the seemingly endless weeds at the base. By this time, not only have the bines accelerated growth in an upward direction, but they have also produced long, snake-like tendrils that wave gracefully in the breeze, and clutch at the necks, faces and arms of the unwary passer-by, i.e. the trainer.

Eventually they grow up and over the tops of the high overhead wires, their foliage creating a jungle-like gloom between the rows. The small green pips that sprout in abundance on them quickly grow into the long, soft green flowers shaped like fir cones. When they are ripe, in September, they are picked, roasted in the

oasthouse kilns, and pressed tightly into long bags to be transported to the breweries. We did not see the whole operation
through (for which, I might add, we were more than grateful!), as it
was time to return to threshing before they were ready to begin
picking.

As we recounted the sordid details of our summer trials and
tribulations to Mr Johnson, he, who had apparently done very little
while we tore our way through the summer, made a joke. "I could
see as soon as you came through that gate this morning that you
were HOPPING MAD!" Very, VERY funny our Mr Johnson! The
horrors of that hop-training summer are still fresh in my mind,
mainly because it made such a deep impression both physically and
mentally. We all really hated it.

I still think that the memories of country people are quite the
most staggering thing. They could take their minds back to quite
trivial incidents that most of us 'townies' would not give a second
thought to. We would listen in astonishment as they argued
whether it was a Monday or a Tuesday that they went somewhere,
or did something, as long as four or five years ago. Farm people
could recall with obvious brain-racking the last time it was "as hot
as this" or "as cold" or "as wet". It seemed to be of vital
importance that they recall the exact date and time of absolutely
everything that ever happened in their lives.

The length and endurance of these memories was well in evidence
at one farm we visited. It was quite a large place, with a spacious
house and plenty of hands to keep things in trim. The farmer was a
genial man in his fifties, with a very pleasant wife and daughter.
The wife's consideration for us could not be faulted; she looked
after the tea arrangements very generously throughout the day, and
was always presenting some offering in the cake, pie or biscuit line.

We were dismayed at the scant respect shown to her by the locals,
even Bill and Bert referring to her in a derogatory manner. They all
called her 'The house-maid'. It did not take much probing to
uncover the 'awful truth' behind this. As a girl, Frances had been
employed as the house-maid to the farmer's family. She had been
wooed and won by the only son of the farmer, and when he
eventually inherited his father's farm, she had of course been
elevated to the status of the farm wife. In the eyes of the local
community, however, she had 'set her cap at him' and 'ruthlessly
trapped him' into the marriage, which put her way above her

natural station in life. The fact that she was an excellent wife and mother, and that they were obviously a very happy family, influenced these rural 'judges' not one iota. She would be called, with barely veiled contempt, 'the house-maid' for the rest of her days.

The lady's cooking was superb, and when we had scoffed our way through a plateful of the most delicious sponge cakes one day, we asked her the secret ingredient that made everything taste so very good. "It's the eggs," she told us, "I always use my ducks' eggs." We had not had a lot to do with duck eggs (London shops sold only the chicken variety) and we wondered aloud what the difference was. "Oh!" said the lady, "There isn't all that much difference with ORDINARY ducks, except that the eggs are stronger in flavour. It is MY birds that produce such wonderfully rich eggs, because I throw all the excess butter from the daily churning into the pond, and they gobble it up like gold-dust." Thinking of the measly two ounce butter ration allocated to us ordinary mortals, while dear Frances was feeding pounds of the precious stuff to her ducks every day, made us feel quite sick, I do not think any of us enjoyed the results of 'the house-maid's' expertise in the kitchen as much after that.

Not many of the farms could provide a full complement of labour for threshing, and sometimes two or three farmers would pool all their resources, lending and borrowing men among themselves as the thresher progressed between their farms. Our advent made so many extra jobs to be done that there were rarely enough hands to cope comfortably. We were very surprised upon arriving at one farm to see a veritable swarm of manpower milling around — there must have been at least a dozen extra hands. As usual, we had to busy ourselves straight away getting everything geared up to start work as quickly as possible, and there was no time to take notice of anyone until the mid-morning teabreak. Then we saw the uniforms of the helpers and realised they were Italian prisoners of war.

It was obvious they were full of curiosity about us, for I do not think they had recognised us as women while we were working. From the little I had heard, their own womenfolk were not seriously involved in men's work, war or no war. They were all fascinated by Valerie, who was fair and very good-looking. She looked them over, but found that the young Romeos, though very handsome, spoke no English at all. It was only two older, much less interesting ones who could communicate a little, so our Valerie lost interest in them!

The one who seemed to be in charge, a round little man of about forty, was fairly well spoken. He told me how weary they all were of a war they had never wanted any part in in the first place, and how they longed to get back to their families. He had a wife and four children that he had not seen for over a year. It was almost impossible to regard them as our 'enemies'. They were just ordinary little people, whose involvement in the conflict was brought upon them, as it was with most of us. Dino had been a shoe-maker in a small town near Turin. Among his companions were a baker, a waiter, two taxi drivers, three students and a shop assistant.

Apart from the odd word or two with Dino at break times, I had very little contact with the others. But, on the last day, as we were finishing the final tasks of disassembling the thresher ready to move on to the next farm, Mario the baker came up to me, took my hand in both of his and, feeling the calluses with unexpectedly gentle fingers he looked up at the bleak winter sky and across at the threshing gear, and stammered in very poor English, "So cold! So hard for ladies!"

Chapter 26

As the long war years continued people grew very weary. We read of bombings and counter-bombings, and as we watched our heavies pass over on their way across the Channel we wished them luck with their targets, and a safe return. Sometimes they trailed flimsy-looking gliders carrying troops, the tow-lines appearing as fragile as spiders' silk, and hardly adequate to keep them from the cold waters of the English Channel.

Food rationing, shortages, the separation from families and worries about the safety of those we loved — all made it difficult to keep hopes up. There were rumours of victories here and invasion there, but official confirmation was lacking. Six years was, after all, a long time to keep a brave smile on one's face, and everyone was afraid to hope. It would have been just too devastating to be disappointed again.

We on the threshing machine were feeling unsettled. Our incentive to 'Go all out for the war effort' seemed to be wavering as the end became tantalisingly close. When eventually the day came that we knew we were working our last farm, it all seemed very unreal.

Mr Johnson was like a cat on hot bricks, and Jo suggested he must already be dusting off the brolly, bowler and brief case in his mind. He did not find he had a meeting to attend, or an urgent phone call to make, but stayed with us all morning and, when we stopped at mid-day, invited us all to go to the pub down the lane from the farm for a drink.

The farmer and all his men came too and, by the time everyone had treated everyone else, we were all extremely merry! I do not know how we coped with that last bit of threshing after such a binge but, somehow, the last stack of corn dwindled down to the end. We packed up the gear for the last time, then, leaning on our bikes as we watched the battered old machines trundle off up the road behind a jubilantly waving Mr Johnson, we were assailed quite unexpectedly with nostalgia.

Of course we were glad it was over at long last as far as we were concerned, and the thought of getting our lives back to normal

after so long was absolutely marvellous. But at the back of our minds we questioned whether this was possible, and I for one had serious doubts. Of the six years of the war, almost five had been spent away from home, and in that time I had changed very much. Stronger mentally as well as physically, I had learned to stand on my own two feet. The naively frivolous teenager had grown up, and the new me, an independent, down-to-earth adult, wondered how I could return to life as a civilian.

I had grown to appreciate the country ways, to know the satisfaction of feeling really tired after a good hard day's work, and I had acquired a new trait to my character, tolerance. Even the awfulness of those first weeks with the Suet family, now that I had seen how very poor was the pay of the labourers on farms, was more understandable. There were many 'Mrs Suets' struggling to feed large families on very small incomes, and I could well understand the temptation of the extra cash we represented. The only knowledge they had of Londoners was through their brief contacts with the hop pickers, and having observed their acceptance of life in those 'piggerzootz', the country people must have had as false a conception of us as we had had of them. Poor Mrs Suet probably imagined she was offering us unaccustomed luxury in that depressing bedroom, and with those 'filling' meals!

I thought of kind, homely Mrs Bird, and how she would soon be losing her welcome lodgers, so that she would have no one to appreciate her delicious meals, or come to her with their problems. I was terribly afraid that life for her would revert to being lonely again.

I would have to say goodbye to this ramshackle old wreck I was leaning on. It had stood me in good stead, and carried me safely over many country miles.

My sturdy shoes, scratched and scuffed, unrecognisable as leather now, were comfortable to the feet that used to be squeezed into flimsy, fashion stilettos, and the multi-patched dungarees, grease-stained and coated with dust, sat comfortably on the strong, almost boyish frame that had once worn those cheap little dresses to the factory. I had, because of my growth and the lack of clothing coupons, worn uniform constantly for all those years, and could no longer imagine myself in feminine garb.

In the beginning, the uniform had been the source of ridicule and an acute embarrassment to wear, but now I was going to miss every part of it. We had been issued with coupons to re-equip ourselves for civilian life, and had to return all our uniform to the Women's Land Army authority, though what they could use it for goodness only knew, most of it was only fit for the rag bag.

I wished I could have kept some part of it as a symbol of such a large slice out of my life, and my pride in the knowledge of a job well done. Had I been given a choice, it would have been difficult to decide, but I reckon in the end it would have had to be those baggy brown breeches and, of course, the shapeless cowboy hat.

Meresborough Books

17 Station Road, Rainham, Gillingham, Kent. ME8 7RS
Telephone: Medway (0634) 388812

We are a specialist publisher of books about Kent. Our books are available in most bookshops in the county, including our own at this address. Alternatively you may order direct, adding 10% for post (minimum 50p, orders over £30 post free). ISBN prefix 0 905270 for 3 figure numbers, 094819 for 4 figure numbers. Titles in print December 1992.

HARDBACKS

AIRCRAFT CASUALTIES IN KENT Part One 1939-40 compiled by G.G. Baxter, K.A. Owen and P. Baldock. ISBN 3506. £12.95.

BARGEBUILDING ON THE SWALE by Don Sattin. ISBN 3530. £9.95.

EDWARDIAN CHISLEHURST by Arthur Battle. ISBN 3433. £9.95.

FISHERMEN FROM THE KENTISH SHORE by Derek Coombe. ISBN 3409. £10.95.

THE HISTORY OF THE ROYAL SEA BATHING HOSPITAL, MARGATE 1791-1991 by F.G. St Clair Strange. ISBN 3573. £12.95.

JUST OFF THE SWALE by Don Sattin. ISBN 045. £5.95.

KENT: A PORTRAIT IN COLOUR by John Guy. ISBN 3700. £12.95.

KENT'S OWN by Robin J. Brooks. The history of 500 (County of Kent) Squadron of the R.A.A.F. ISBN 541. £5.95.

THE LONDON, CHATHAM & DOVER RAILWAY by Adrian Gray. ISBN 886. £7.95.

A NEW DICTIONARY OF KENT DIALECT by Alan Major. ISBN 274. £7.50.

THE PAST GLORY OF MILTON CREEK by Alan Cordell and Leslie Williams. ISBN 3042. £9.95.

THE PLACE NAMES OF KENT by Judith Glover. ISBN 614. £7.50. BARGAIN OFFER £4.95.

ROCHESTER FROM OLD PHOTOGRAPHS compiled by the City of Rochester Society. Large format. ISBN 975. £7.95.(Also available in paperback ISBN 983. £4.95.)

SHERLOCK HOLMES AND THE KENT RAILWAYS by Kelvin Jones. ISBN 3255. £8.95.

A SIDEWAYS LAUNCH by Anne Salmon. ISBN 3689. £15.95.

STRATFORD HOUSE SCHOOL 1912-1987 by Susan Pittman. ISBN 3212. £10.00.

TALES OF VICTORIAN HEADCORN or The Oddities of Heddington by Penelope Rivers (Ellen M. Poole). ISBN 3050. £8.95. (Also available in paperback ISBN 3069. £3.95).

TEYNHAM MANOR AND HUNDRED (798-1935) by Elizabeth Selby, MBE. ISBN 630. £5.95.

TROOPSHIP TO CALAIS by Derek Spiers. ISBN 3395. £11.95.

TWO HALVES OF A LIFE by Doctor Kary Pole. ISBN 509. £5.95.

US BARGEMEN by A.S. Bennett. ISBN 207. £6.95.

A VIEW OF CHRIST'S COLLEGE, BLACKHEATH by A.E.O. Crombie, B.A. ISBN 223. £6.95.

LARGE FORMAT PICTORIAL PAPERBACKS

ARE YOU BEING SERVED, MADAM? by Molly Proctor. ISBN 3174. £3.50.

BEFORE AND AFTER THE HURRICANE IN AND AROUND CANTERBURY by Paul Crampton. ISBN 3387. £3.50. BARGAIN £1.95.

THE BLITZ OF CANTERBURY by Paul Crampton. ISBN 3441. £3.50.

CANTERBURY BEFORE THE BLITZ by Paul Crampton. ISBN 3662. £4.95.

CANTERBURY THEN AND NOW by Paul Crampton. ISBN 359X. £3.95.

CLIFFE IN OLD PHOTOGRAPHS by Allan Cherry. ISBN 362X. £3.95.

EAST KENT FROM THE AIR by John Guy. ISBN 3158. £3.50.
EAST SUSSEX RAILWAYS IN OLD POSTCARDS by Kevin Robertson. ISBN 3220. £3.50.
GEORGE BARGEBRICK Esq. by Richard-Hugh Perks. ISBN 479. £4.50.
HEADCORN: A Pictorial History by the Headcorn Local History Society. ISBN 3271. £3.50.
KENT TOWN CRAFTS by Richard Filmer. ISBN 584. £2.95.
LENHAM AND BOUGHTON MALHERBE IN OLD PHOTOGRAPHS by Jean Cockett and Amy Myers. ISBN 3646. £3.95.
THE LIFE AND ART OF ONE MAN by Dudley Pout. ISBN 525. £2.95.
THE MEDWAY TOWNS FROM THE AIR by Piers Morgan and Diane Nicholls. ISBN 3557. £4.95.
MORE PICTURES OF RAINHAM by Barbara Mackay Miller. ISBN 3298. £3.50.
THE MOTOR BUS SERVICES OF KENT AND EAST SUSSEX — A brief history by Eric Baldock. ISBN 959. £4.95.
OLD BROADSTAIRS by Michael David Mirams. ISBN 3115. £3.50.
OLD CHATHAM: A THIRD PICTURE BOOK by Philip MacDougall. ISBN 3190. £3.50. BARGAIN £1.95.
OLD FAVERSHAM by Arthur Percival. ISBN 3425. £3.50.
OLD GILLINGHAM by Philip MacDougall. ISBN 3328. £3.50.
OLD MAIDSTONE Vol.3 by Irene Hales. ISBN 3336. £3.50. BARGAIN £1.95.
OLD MARGATE by Michael David Mirams. ISBN 851. £3.50.
OLD PUBS OF TUNBRIDGE WELLS & DISTRICT by Keith Hetherington and Alun Griffiths. ISBN 300X. £3.50.
OLD RAMSGATE by Michael David Mirams. ISBN 797. £3.50.
PEMBURY IN THE PAST by Mary Standen. ISBN 916. £2.95.
A PICTORIAL HISTORY OF COOLING AND CLIFFE by Allan Cherry. ISBN 376X. £3.95.
A PICTORIAL STUDY OF ALKHAM PARISH by Susan Lees and Roy Humphreys. ISBN 3034. £2.95.
A PICTORIAL STUDY OF HAWKINGE PARISH by Roy Humphreys. ISBN 328X. £3.50.
A PICTUREBOOK OF OLD NORTHIAM by Lis Rigby. ISBN 3492. £3.95.
A PICTUREBOOK OF OLD RAINHAM by Barbara Mackay Miller. ISBN 606. £3.50.
REMINISCENCES OF OLD CRANBROOK by Joe Woodcock. ISBN 331X. £3.50.
ROCHESTER FROM OLD PHOTOGRAPHS — see under hardbacks.
SMARDEN: A Pictorial History by Jenni Rodger. ISBN 592. £3.50.
STEAM SCENE AT TONBRIDGE by Mike Feaver. ISBN 3670. £3.95.
THOMAS SIDNEY COOPER OF CANTERBURY by Brian Stewart. ISBN 762. £2.95.
TRANSPORT IN KENT 1900-1938 by Eric Baldock. ISBN 3603. £3.95.
WEST KENT FROM THE AIR by John Guy. ISBN 3166. £3.50.

STANDARD SIZE PAPERBACKS

BIRDS OF KENT: A Review of their Status and Distribution by the Kent Ornithological Society. ISBN 800. £6.95.
BIRDWATCHING IN KENT by Don Taylor. ISBN 932. £4.50.
THE CANTERBURY MONSTERS by John H. Vaux. ISBN 3468. £2.50.
THE CHATHAM DOCKYARD STORY by Philip MacDougall. ISBN 3301. £6.95.
CHIDDINGSTONE — AN HISTORICAL EXPLORATION by Jill Newton. ISBN 940. £1.95.
A CHRONOLOGY OF ROCHESTER by Brenda Purle. ISBN 851. £1.50.
THE CHURCH AND VILLAGE OF TUNSTALL by Arthur A. Midwinter. ISBN 3697. £3.95.
COBHAM. Published for Cobham Parish Council. ISBN 3123. £1.00.
CRIME AND CRIMINALS IN VICTORIAN KENT by Adrian Gray. ISBN 967. £3.95.

CYCLE TOURS OF KENT by John Guy. No. 1: Medway, Gravesend, Sittingbourne and Sheppey. ISBN 517. £1.50.
EXPLORING KENT CHURCHES by John E. Vigar. ISBN 3018. £3.95.
EXPLORING SUSSEX CHURCHES by John E. Vigar. ISBN 3093. £3.95.
FLIGHT IN KENT. ISBN 3085. £1.95.
FROM MOTHS TO MERLINS: The History of West Malling Airfield by Robin J. Brooks. ISBN 3239. £4.95.
THE GHOSTS OF KENT by Peter Underwood. ISBN 86X. £3.95.
HAWKINGE 1912-1961 by Roy Humphreys. ISBN 3522. £8.95.
A HISTORY OF CHATHAM GRAMMAR SCHOOL FOR GIRLS, 1907-1982 by Audrey Perkyns. ISBN 576. £1.95.
THE HOP BIN by Geoff & Fran Doel. ISBN 3735. £5.95.
IN BAGGY BROWN BREECHES by Norah Turner. ISBN 3654. £4.95.
KENT AIRFIELDS IN THE BATTLE OF BRITAIN by the Kent Aviation Historical Research Society. ISBN 3247. £5.95.
KENT AND EAST SUSSEX UNDERGROUND by The Kent Underground Research Group. ISBN 3581. £5.95.
KENT COUNTRY CHURCHES by James Antony Syms. ISBN 3131. £4.50.
KENT COUNTRY CHURCHES CONTINUED by James Antony Syms. ISBN 314X. £5.95.
KENT COUNTRY CHURCHES CONCLUDED by James Antony Syms. ISBN 345X. £5.95.
KENT INNS AND SIGNS by Michael David Mirams. ISBN 3182. BARGAIN £2.50.
LET'S EXPLORE THE RIVER DARENT by Frederick Wood. ISBN 770. £1.95.
LETTER TO MARSHY by Barbara Trigg. ISBN 3727. £3.95.
LULLINGSTONE PARK: THE EVOLUTION OF A MEDIAEVAL DEER PARK by Susan Pittman. ISBN 703. £3.95.
MARDEN: A WEALDEN VILLAGE by Phyllis Highwood and Peggy Skelton. ISBN 3107. £4.95.
MUMMING, HOWLING AND HOODENING by Geoff & Fran Doel. ISBN 3743. £3.50.
OFF THE BEATEN TRACK by Geoffrey Hufton. ISBN 3751. £3.50.
ONE DOG AND HER MAN by Ted Wright. ISBN 3719. £5.95.
PENINSULA ROUND (The Hoo Peninsula) by Des Worsdale. ISBN 568. £1.50.
PRELUDE TO WAR: Aviation in Kent 1938-39 by KAHRS. ISBN 3476. £2.50.
RADIO KENT GARDENERS' GUIDE by Harry Smith and Bob Collard. ISBN 3549. £3.95.
SAINT ANDREW'S CHURCH, DEAL by Gregory Holyoake. ISBN 835. 95p.
THE SCHOOL ON THE BALL FIELDS (CRANBROOK) by Mary Standen. ISBN 3638. £5.95.
SHORNE: The History of a Kentish Village by A.F. Allen. ISBN 3204. £4.95.
SIR GARRARD TYRWHITT-DRAKE AND THE COBTREE ESTATE, MAIDSTONE by Elizabeth Melling B.A. ISBN 3344. £1.50.
SITTINGBOURNE & KEMSLEY LIGHT RAILWAY STOCKBOOK AND GUIDE. ISBN 843. 95p.
STEAM IN MY FAMILY by John Newton. ISBN 3417. £4.95.
STOUR VALLEY WALKS from Canterbury to Sandwich by Christopher Donaldson. ISBN 991. £1.95.
TALES OF VICTORIAN HEADCORN — see under hardbacks.
TARGET FOLKESTONE by Roy Humphreys. ISBN 3514. £7.95.
WADHURST: Town of the High Weald by Alan Savidge and Oliver Mason. ISBN 3352. £5.95.
WARTIME KENT 1939-40 compiled by Oonagh Hyndman from the BBC Radio Kent broadcasts. ISBN 3611. £6.95.
WHERE NO FLOWERS GROW by George Glazebrook. ISBN 3379. £2.50.
WHO'S BURIED WHERE IN KENT by Alan Major. ISBN 3484. £5.95.